Signs, Science and Symbols of the Prophecy

Andrew the Prophet

Andrew The Prophet, LLC
Denver, CO

Signs, Science and Symbols of the Prophecy
Andrew the Prophet

Copyright © 2008 by Andrew the Prophet, LLC

Printed in the United States of America

These words are dedicated to

His Witnesses

Purchased by the Blood of Our Lord

Contents

Prelude: The Opening Call To
Andrew the Prophet
Completed December 31, 2007

Ezekiel was instructed to lie on his side for 410 days, and the siege of Jerusalem would last for exactly 410 days. Quod erat demonstradum "which was to be shown". For the proof lies in the result. The dates have been set in motion, many of which are not disclosed, for they are dates that men should not know. But one thing that man does know, is the universe that we live in.

Solo scriptura. The contemporary biblical view that the proof should lie within the scripture. However the Bible was written by the hands of men, and not by the hands of God ...for if this were true, we would have the Gospel according to Jesus, and still have the tablets from Mount Sinai. And many other religions have words that were inspired from God. Thus the Bible has been subject to the faults of man, and other religions have been subject to the inspiration of the Spirit. Yet the Bible is a divinely inspired work, inspired by the Holy Spirit. And the fault of other religions, is they fail to know that Christ is God. For He came as a man to save all mankind. But Christ is not just a man. For He is One in Three: THE HOLY TRINITY.

Solo physiologia. The view that the proof lies within all of nature, within the scientific properties of this universe. For too long has there been enmity between science and religion, for they are one and the same. Science is faulted for not recognizing that science imitates theology. And theology is faulted for not realizing that nature *objectively* imitates God.

Signs and symbols. The signs and symbols abound during these times. But man in his ignorance fails to recognize them. For this world is a faulted image of His perfect kingdom. But look at the symbols and the signs, and appreciate the beauty and the glory of the kingdom to come.

I believe that these words are inspired by the Spirit, but are subject to the hands of a man. And not just a man but one with many faults. But if the words are true then *Quod erat demonstradum*. The results will be shown.

The proposition is that the end times are upon us.
The proof is the words which inspire these words.
And the result, if this is true, may God help us all.

ατπ

I

"I am the way, the truth, and the life. No one comes to the Father except through Me." John 14:6

What does π look like? π is a gate, the design upon which the temples were built. And π is an infinite and transcendental number, a number not understood in finite mortal terms. And Einstein said that if he could comprehend π, then he could comprehend God, for π is the number of God. And it truly is. And what does π look like? It is the narrow gate, for it represents Christ who is the Gate. And do you remember what He said on the Mount? "Enter through the narrow gate; for the gate is wide and the way is broad that leads to destruction, and there are many who enter through it. For the gate is small and the way is narrow that leads to life, and there are few who find it." (Matthew 7:12-13) For we all were created by the Father, and we all have fallen away from the Father. But Christ interceded on our behalf, and gave us the gateway to return to the Father. But to complete the circle back to the Father, we must go through Christ who is the narrow Gate. And what is the formula to complete the circle? The formula of circumference = $\pi \cdot$ diameter. Circumference is the path to return to the Father, and diameter is the distance you are away from the Father. And Solomon was told when he constructed the temple, that the value of π was equal to 3, "ten cubits from one brim to the other; it was completely round... and a line of thirty cubits measured its circumference." (1 Kings 7:23). And obviously that answer was far from complete. For many have come close, but no one on their own has returned to the Father. For this is humanly impossible, for π is an infinite number. Until Christ

1

the Son came down to mankind, for He is the Gate "the way, the truth, and the life. No one can go to the Father except through Me." (John 14:6) **Christ is π.** When we go through Him, then we return to the Father. But no one can return to the Father except through Him!

Christ = π = The Narrow Gate

Circumference = π • diameter Circumference

= path back to the Father

diameter = distance between you & the Father

π = 3.14159265358979238472743383279502884197169399375105820 09840445023781...∞

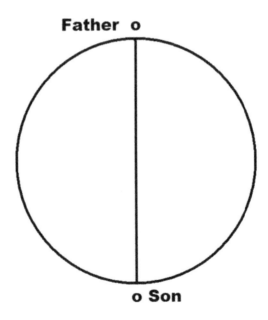

And the circular pattern above is a symbol commonly used in India. For the pattern represents karma, "what goes around, comes around"! All have come from the Father, and all will return to the Father. Amen. All men.

II

The Antichrist is Here, The King Returns (NASB)
To Andrew the Prophet
Completed August 23, 2007

"Then I saw another beast coming up out of the earth; and he had two horns like a lamb and he spoke as a dragon...Here is wisdom. Let him who has understanding calculate the number of the beast, for the number is that of a man; and his number is **six hundred and sixty-six.**"(Revelation 13:11-18)

How the saints have patiently waited, for the King to return! But woe to those who have turned from the Lamb. Although the King returns to save all, He does not return as the Lamb. For He will return as the Lion. And by His iron rod and will, all sins shall be paid in full. For as Christ the Lamb has promised the world, "truly I say to you, you will not come out of there until you have paid up the last cent." (Matthew 5:26). Turn now and confess to the Lamb, for the price of the Lion is just and GREAT.

May 25, 2007: Moqtada al-S̲adr returns from Iran to S̲adr City, Iraq to speak "as a dragon" to his followers, "No, no **Satan**; no, no USA; no, no occupation; no, no Israel". He comes "out of the earth" to be dictator of his country, Iraq, S̲yria of old, Babylon of old, Garden of Eden, the origin of mankind, and the GOG (garden of god). And on that day, 6̲000 S̲hiites listened to him speak, and 6̲ US troops died. And the beast, has a number, *"and his number is 666"*. (Revelation 13:18)

His followers call al-Sadr "the Mahdi", for the Mahdi is the "guided one". He will lead his people against the "infidels", as prophesied by the Shi'a faith. The Mahdi followers, the Mahdi army, prepare the way for the end of this world.

But even if you don't believe prophecies, take a look at these cold hard facts:

1. His followers call him by the revered name "martyr imam"

   A. Imam is reserved for the holiest of holy men in the country. He is the son and the nephew of the two previous Imam Ayatollahs of Iraq. He is also a direct descendant of the prophet Mohammed. **He is the Imam or Grand Ayatollah of Iraq.**

   B. He is called imam martyr because the Bush and Reagan administrations assisted in the assassination of his father, Imam Mohammed Sadiq al-Sadr, and his two brothers in 1999, and the execution of his uncle, Imam Mohammed Baqir al-Sadr, in 1980. During the Iran-Iraq war, the US under Ronald Reagan and George Bush Sr, gave tens of billions of dollars of military support to Saddam Hussein to destroy the Shi'a government. Its leaders at the time were his father Imam Ayatollah Mohammed Sadiq al-Sadr and his uncle Imam Ayatollah Mohammed Baqir al-Sadr. They are now worshiped as the two holiest martyrs of Iraq, the *"two horns of the lamb"* (Revelation 13:11). Al-Sadr is hell bent on avenging the death of his family by the hands of the US government, and he will.

2. His father and uncle studied with Imam Ayatollah Khomeini of Iran, also a direct descendant of the prophet Mohammed. Furthermore, his uncle is Mohammad Khatami, the previous president of Iran. Al-Sadr's Mahdi army is trained by and consists of the Iranian Revolutionary Guards. In other words, the holy and political families of Iran and Iraq are blood relatives! Mahmoud Ahmadinejad, the president of Iran, and Moqtada al-Sadr are very close allies.

3. Iran is much more advanced in nuclear weapons development than the press leads us to believe. In fact, reports show that Iran has over 5000 nuclear centrifuges and recently was able to manufacture tritium, an important fuel for nuclear fusion bombs. And now they have a contract with Russia to supply them with uranium for their "nuclear reactors." And remember, there are 250 "suitcase nuclear bombs" (called RA115s) still missing from Russia after the Iron Curtain came down; and it is widely assumed that al-Qaeda has 50 of them in their possession. (Off the record, a suitcase nuke was recently found in Iraq).

4. Iran is getting their gasoline from President Chavez in Venezuela and their citizens are on gasoline restrictions because their oil reserves are low and they lack the ability to refine their oil.

5. Iraq has the third largest oil supply in the world (at least 20 trillion dollars worth) and they have the refineries to process it, which the US government has been so diligent to protect.

6. Iraq is averaging 2 suicide bombings per day, and the number is rapidly increasing.

7. By conservative estimates, al-Sadr has 4 million faithful followers and an army of over 100,000 troops and has the support of the Iranian Revolutionary Guards.

And what will happen, the answer is simple. For the Shi'a controls both of these "horns", and their blood lines are tied by religion. (Daniel 7) And Iran is assisting with weapons and training. And Iran will run out of their oil, but they do have the means for nuclear warfare. And Iraq has 20 trillion dollars of oil in the fields, but they do not yet have nuclear weapons. Who is to keep them from trading oil for nuclear weapons? And who is going to keep an Iraqi suicide bomber from detonating a nuclear weapon on US soil? And who is securing the Mexican border? Believe me, not Bush, not Cheney, not the US, no one!

And what is the answer? The answer is simple. For the seals have been opened, the trigger has been pulled, and the bomb is ticking away. **But man has no hope to intervene, for God the Father has control in all things**. His prophecy is like a skilled surgeon's knife, perfect and precise, for the judgment of man will lie in His hands.

The question is then not if it will come, for the end will come soon, but what can we do to prepare for the end? Again, the answer is simple. "Thus it is written, that the Christ would suffer and rise again from the dead the third day, and that repentance for forgiveness of sins would be proclaimed in His name to all the nations." (Luke 24:46-47) For we will be judged by the Lamb or the Lion. And Christ the Lamb can forgive your sins, or Christ the Lion can judge for your sins. "Each man's work will become evident; for the day will show it because it is to be revealed with fire, and the fire itself will test the quality of each man's work. If any man's work which he has built on it remains, he will receive a reward. If any man's work is burned up, he will suffer loss; but he himself will be saved, yet so as through fire." (1 Corinthians 3:13-16)

Thus there is still time to ask for forgiveness. For the time of the Lamb is now. The Judgment Day is near. And the Lion will return. So, come Lord Jesus. Come.

III

The Greek Alphabet and God, the Author of Creation (NASB)
To Andrew the Prophet
Completed September 15, 2007

"My heart is overflowing with a good theme; I recite my composition concerning the King; My tongue is the pen of a ready writer." (Psalms 45:1)

α   The Father, The Beginning

(Numerical value = 1)

"In the **beginning** God created the heavens and the earth." (Genesis 1:1)

What is alpha?

It is the first letter of the alphabet and represents the number 1. But more importantly it represents God the Father, the author and the letter of all creation. "'I am the Alpha and the Omega,' says the Lord God, 'who is and who was and who is to come, the Almighty.'" (Revelation 1:8) In the system of Greek numbers, the number 1 represents singleness and unity, just as the Father is Oneness, Unity, and completeness in Himself. For the Father is the all in all. "When all things are subjected to Him, then the Son Himself also will be subjected to the One who subjected all things to Him, so that God may be all in all." (1 Corinthians 15:28)

The symbol also resembles a "fish", the universal symbol for Christianity. The origin of this symbol comes from a Greek translation of the verse, "Jesus Christ, Son of God Savior; Iesous

(IXΘΥΣ). And in His image, He taught His disciples to be fishers of men.

"Follow Me, and I will make you fishers of men." (Matthew 4:19)

Ω   God, The End   (Numerical value = 800)

"'I am the Alpha and the **Omega**,' says the Lord God, 'who is and who was and who is to come, the Almighty.'" (Revelation 1:8)

What is omega?

It is the final letter of the Greek alphabet. But more importantly it represents God, the final and eternal author and letter of creation. "Behold, I am coming quickly, and My reward is with Me, to render to every man according to what he has done. 'I am the Alpha and the Omega, the first and the last, the beginning and the end.'" (Revelation 22:12-13)

It is also the 24th letter of the Greek alphabet, just as God will return in the 24th hour, to destroy Satan and his dominion on earth. "Alas, alas, that great city Babylon, that mighty city! For in one hour your judgment has come." (Revelation 18:10)

And the literal meaning of the word is "great" (*mega - mega meaning* **great**). And it is reflected in the Muslim verse, "God is great". "For You are great and do wondrous deeds; You alone are God." (Psalms 86:10)

Finally what does the symbol look like? For yes, it is a nuclear mushroom! "And I saw something like a sea of glass mixed with fire." (Revelation 15:2)

Π   Christ, The Gate   (Numerical value = 80)

"Enter by the narrow **gate**; for wide is the **gate** and broad is the way that leads to destruction, and there are many who go in by it. Because narrow is the **gate** and difficult is the way which leads to life, and there are few who find it." (Matthew 7:13)

What does Π look like? It is a gate back to the Father, just as Christ is the Way the Truth and the Life, for He is the narrow Gate. Einstein once said that Π was the number of God, and that if he could figure out what Π represented, then He could figure out who God is, because it is the number of God. And it truly is for Christ is the transcendental number Π.

We all originate from the Father, and have fallen away from Him. Christ interceded on our behalf, and gave us the Gate to return to the Father. To complete the circle of life, we must go through Christ the Gate. And what is the formula to complete the circle? It is C = Π • d for circumference, the path back to the Father, is equal to Π times the diameter, the distance between you and the Father. Solomon was commanded by God to build His temple, and was told that Π was equal to 3. "Now he made the sea of cast metal ten cubits from brim to brim... and thirty cubits in circumference."(1 Kings 7:23). And obviously, that was nowhere close to returning to the Father. And there are now computers programs, that calculate the value of Π to millions of decimal places, yet they are all wrong. Many have come close, but none has returned to the Father on their own accord, because Π is infinite and man is not. That is until Christ came. For He is the Way the Truth and the Life, for He is the narrow Gate. No one can go to the Father except through Him. When we go through Him, then we will return to the Father. **No one can return to the Father except through Him!**

And what does this symbol represent? This represents theta (θ) the symbol of the Son of God. (more on theta at a future date)

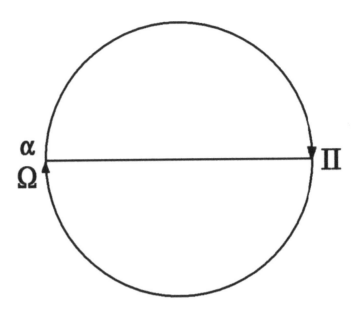

"I am the way, and the truth, and the life; no one comes to the Father but through Me." (John 14:14)

ι   Iota, The Holy Spirit   (Numerical value = 10)

"But the Helper, the **Holy Spirit**, whom the Father will send in My name, He will teach you all things, and bring to your remembrance all things that I said to you." (John 14:26)

Iota is a beautiful number, because like the Holy Spirit, it may appear insignificant and is often invisible, but in actuality is ubiquitous and powerful. "Where can I go from Your Spirit? Or where can I flee from Your presence? If I ascend to heaven, You are there; If I make my bed in Sheol, behold, You are there. If I take the wings of the dawn, If I dwell in the remotest part of the sea, Even there Your hand will lead me, And Your right hand will lay hold of me. If I say, 'Surely the darkness will overwhelm me, And the light around me will be night,' Even the darkness is not dark to You, And the night is as bright as the day. Darkness and light are alike to You." (Psalms 139:7-12)

Iota may be the smallest letter of the Greek alphabet, but in Greek numerals iota represents the powerful value of 10. The number ten represents perfection and productivity. In like manner, the Holy Spirit is God's perfection, and gives His servants great productivity. In mathematics, it is the root of our numerical system. The reason for this choice is assumed to be that humans have ten fingers or digits. The number 10 is a powerful and productive number because the value of any integer can be increased ten fold simply by adding a zero to the end of it. And interestingly, the Chinese numeral for ten is $+$ which resembles a cross. And of course, the number 10 is repeated throughout the history of God. For the Israelites were instructed to give one-tenth of their produce to God, and God's finger wrote on stone the Ten Commandments, and God inflicted Egypt with Ten Plagues. Therefore, just as the iota represents numerical power, perfection and productivity, the Holy Spirit represents Godly power and perfection and spiritual productivity. In other words, the gifts of the Spirit produce great power through the fruits of our labor. "For our gospel did not come to you in word only, but also in power and in the Holy Spirit." (1 Thessalonians 1:5)

Iota is also used as a marker of pronunciation by diphthongs. Before the development of the classical Greek alphabet, there was no way of distinguishing between long and short vowels. Thus diphthongs, or iotas, were added to the words to distinguish the pronunciation of these vowels. And these iotas can now be seen throughout various languages including the Czech, Dutch, English, Faroese, Finnish, French, German, Hungarian, Icelandic, Italian, Latvian, Northern Sami, Norwegian, Portuguese, Romanian, and Spanish languages. So just as the iota has ubiquitously influenced the pronunciation of many languages, so has the Holy Spirit ubiquitously penetrated the voice of all the nations. "But whatever is given you in that hour, speak that; for it is not you who speak, but the Holy Spirit." (Mark 13:11) "And they were all filled with the Holy Spirit and began to speak with other tongues, as the Spirit gave them utterance." (Acts 2:4)

The iota has also penetrated the written languages and the artistry of the world. The iota was written as an 'iota subscript' in the original languages. The 'iota subscript' is a way of writing the letter iota as a small vertical stroke beneath a vowel. Eventually, they became incorporated as serifs, or non-structural details, on the ends of strokes that make up letters and symbols.

For example:

CHRIST = no serif **CHRIST** = serif

These embellishments were also incorporated into the Asian and Aramaic written languages. Thus, just as the iota has penetrated all the written and artistic languages, so has the Holy Spirit penetrated the written and artistic languages of all the nations. "And I have filled him with the Spirit of God, in wisdom, in understanding, in knowledge, and in all manner of workmanship, to design artistic works, to work in gold, in silver, in bronze, in cutting jewels for setting, in carving wood, and to work in all manner of workmanship." (Exodus 31:3-5) And like the letter of the languages of the nations, our hearts have become the letter of the Spirit. "You are our letter, written in our hearts, known and read by all men; being manifested that you are a letter of Christ, cared for by us, written not with ink but with the Spirit of the living God, not on tablets of stone but on tablets of human hearts." (2 Corinthians 3:2-3)

"For assuredly, I say to you, till heaven and earth pass away, one jot or one tittle will by no means pass from the law till all is fulfilled." (Matthew 5:18) And this is the one scriptural passage that directly refers to the letter iota. "Jot" translates to "iota" in Greek, and is paraphrased as "not one iota of difference". This was the foundation of the theological debate at the First Council of Nicaea regarding the nature of the Trinity. The argument centered on which of two Greek words, differing only by a single "iota", should be used to distinguish Jesus' relationship in the Holy Trinity. One word "homoousious" meant that Jesus was of the same substance as God the Father, and the other "homo**i**ousious" meant that Jesus was of a similar substance. The verdict, of course, was that they are "homoousious". **They are all of the same substance ...the Father, the Son, and the Holy Spirit are Three in One: the Holy Trinity.**

And the numerical values of the Greek symbols that pertain to the Trinity are as follows:

$$\alpha = 1$$

$$\Pi = 80$$

$$\iota = 10$$

$$\Omega = 800$$

If the Trinity is One, then $\Omega = \alpha \cdot \Pi \cdot \iota$
$$800 = 1 \cdot 80 \cdot 10$$
$$800 = 800$$

Thus, the Father, Son, and Holy Spirit are One

Finally in mathematics, the imaginary unit, iota, allows the real numerical system to be extended into the complex numerical system. Real numbers are those numbers that can be represented by "real" numerical values; in other words, numbers that exist in the "real world". Complex numbers are also called imaginary numbers, and represent those numbers that were once thought to be nonexistent, but presently are utilized to understand quantum physics and the theory of relativity. The numerical value of an imaginary unit is:

$$\iota = \sqrt{-1}$$

which is an impossible value by real number mathematics.

In other words, they are numbers that presently do not exist in our physical world, but do exist in another realm (a parallel universe); a realm that we do not yet understand. Thus, as the imaginary unit, iota, in mathematics is used to transcend numbers from a real set of values into an imaginary set of values, so does the Holy Spirit transcend mankind from the mortal realm of this earth, to the eternal realm of the Father's kingdom. "Immediately I was in the Spirit; and behold, a throne was standing in heaven, and One sitting on the throne." (Revelations 2:4)

And Remember This Formula For the Future

EULER'S FORMULA

$$e^{\iota\pi} + 1 = 0$$

Solve this formula and you unlock the mysteries of God and the universe!

I V

God is Water, the Sustenance of Life (NKJV)
To Andrew the Prophet
Completed August 22, 2007

God created water to sustain the earth

"And God called the dry land Earth, and the gathering together of the **waters** He called Seas. And God saw that it was good." Genesis 1:10

"Then God said, "Let the **waters** abound with an abundance of living creatures, and let birds fly above the earth across the face of the firmament of the heavens."" Genesis 1:20

"Now a river went out of Eden to **water** the garden, and from there it parted and became four riverheads." Genesis 2:10

"You visit the earth and water it, You greatly enrich it; The river of God is full of **water**; You provide their grain, For so You have prepared it." Psalms 65:9

God the Father is the Water of life, our Sustenance

"Jesus answered, "Most assuredly, I say to you, unless one is born of **water** and the Spirit, he cannot enter the kingdom of God."" John 3:5

"He who believes in Me, as the Scripture has said, out of his heart will flow rivers of living **water**." John 7:38

"And there are three that bear witness on earth: the Spirit, the **water**, and the blood; and these three agree as one."1 John 5:8

The Water will dwell amongst us forever

"Jesus answered and said to her, "Whoever drinks of this **water** will thirst again, "but whoever drinks of the water that I shall give him will never thirst. But the water that I shall give him will become in him a fountain of water springing up into everlasting life."" John 4:13

"And He said to me, "It is done! I am the Alpha and the Omega, the Beginning and the End. I will give of the fountain of the **water** of life freely to him who thirsts."" Revelation 21:6

"And he showed me a pure river of **water** of life, clear as crystal, proceeding from the throne of God and of the Lamb. In the middle of its street, and on either side of the river, was the tree of life, which bore twelve fruits, each tree yielding its fruit every month. And the leaves of the tree were for the healing of the nations." Revelation 22:1

The Father is Water

Symbolism is allegorical and beautiful. And God gave us symbols to represent, that which we cannot understand, and that is the infinite spectrum of the Father, and the heavens and the earth He created. And the greatest symbolism is not in man's words, but the greatest symbolism is in creation itself. "For behold, He who forms mountains, And creates the wind, Who declares to man what his thought is, And makes the morning darkness, Who treads the high places of the earth--The Lord God of hosts is His name." (Amos 4:13)

And God created the water of the earth (Genesis 1:10), and from these waters all living things grew. (Genesis 1:20) And in the garden of Adam and Eve, the riverheads flowed with its sustaining life. (Genesis 2:10) For from that water the gardens grew grain, the bread that sustained their comfort and life. (Psalms 65:9)

And water can form complex hydrogen bonds, so biochemical

each other, even the simplest life process is impossible. And the Father is sustenance and water, for He allows all things to work together in harmony. For "we know that all things work together for good to those who love God, to those who are the called according to His purpose." (Romans 8:28)

Water is a sustaining and cleansing fluid. It removes the debris and waste products from biological systems. And God is sustenance and cleansing. He is the sustenance of life, for all things exist through Him. And He is cleansing for mankind. For He sent His only Son to bring us the Word of God, and to shed His blood for man, that we may receive the Holy Spirit. For as the Lord said, we must be born of water, confessing our sins to Christ, and relying on the sustenance of the Father. And having cleansed our temples, we receive the Holy Spirit, that we may enter the kingdom of God. (John 3:5) And now that the Spirit dwells in us, "the rivers of living water" can flow from us. (John 7:38)

Water is supportive for any living organism. It allows the plants to support their stems. And our bodies consist of two-thirds water. Thus water gives our body structure, form, and strength. And the Father is our support and strength. He sustains our life and fulfills our needs. He gives us the spiritual guidance and strength, to weather the trials and storms. For the Father is the water which never fails. "The LORD will guide you always; he will satisfy your needs in a sun-scorched land and will strengthen your frame. You will be like a well-watered garden, like a spring whose waters never fail." (Isaiah 58:11)

Water exists in three different forms: vapor, water, and ice. Though they are the same substance, they exist in three different forms. Just as the Trinity is one God, but exists in three separate forms. And vapor is the breath of the Holy Spirit. "The Spirit of God has made me, And the breath of the Almighty gives me life." (Job 33:4) And ice is the rock of Christ, the cornerstone of the Church. "For they drank of that spiritual Rock that followed them, and that Rock was Christ." (1 Corinthians 10:4) And water is the sustenance from the Father, the sustenance and structure of creation. "You visit the earth

21

and water it, You greatly enrich it; The river of God is full of water" (Psalms 65:9) "And there are three that bear witness on earth: the Spirit, the water (the Father), and the blood (the Son); and these three agree as one."(1 John 5:8)

And speaking of its structure, the molecule of water is a trinity. For it consists of three separate atoms: two hydrogens and one oxygen. Oxygen symbolizes the Spirit, for the Spirit is the breath of life. And hydrogen symbolizes the Father, and hydrogen in the likeness of the Father is the Son. And the Son exists in unity with the Father, for as the Son said of the Father, "I and My Father are one." (John 10:30) And what if you fuse the Father and the Son? And what happens if you fuse hydrogen? Remember the holocaust of Hiroshima and Nagasaki? For what you get is the result of the hydrogen bomb, the prototype of the nuclear bomb. **The catastrophic release of energy is a result of fusing the Father and the Son into One!**

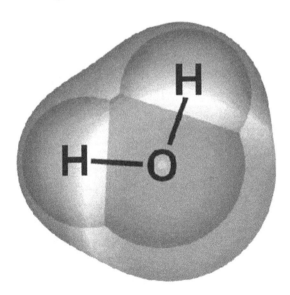

And now that we enter the end of this world, we will better understand the mysteries of the Trinity. For as we do know, it is impossible to divide one into three. (1 divided by 3 = 0.333333333.......∞). But for _____ symbolism He has shown us.

But once the wrath of God, the payment of sins, and the reconciliation of man to the Father is complete, then all men will drink from the Water of life. And man will never be thirsty again, for the Water will flow freely for all. (Revelation 21:6) And man will never again suffer, for the Living Water shall heal the nations. (Revelation 22:1)

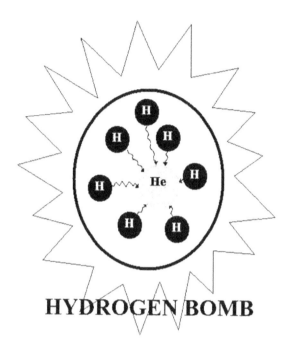

HYDROGEN BOMB

The First Hydrogen Bomb

The first hydrogen bomb was detonated on November 1, 1952 at the Marshall Islands. The blast produced a light greater than 1,000 suns and a heat wave that was felt over 50 kilometers away. Documentation from the Department of Energy states: "The immense ball of flame, cloud of dust, evaporated steel tower, melted sand for 1000 feet, 10 million tons of water rising out of the lagoon, waves subsiding from a height of 80 feet to seven feet in three miles, were all repeated in varying degrees, 43 times at Enewetak" Sound familiar? "And I saw something like a sea of glass mingled with fire, and those who have the victory over the beast, over his image and over his mark and over the number of his name, standing on the sea of glass, having harps of God." (Revelation 15:2)

Five islands in the atoll were completely vaporized by the testing. Nearly all the vegetation was destroyed, and half of the atoll remains uninhabitable. Thousands of Marshall Islanders were evacuated. An unknown number perished from starvation and radiation poisoning. But ultimately, the human toll is immeasurable.

V

Christ is Light (NKJV) To
Andrew the Prophet
Completed August 22, 2007

"I am the **light** of the world. He who follows Me shall not walk in darkness, but have the **light** of life." John 8:12

God is Light and Darkness

"The darkness and the **light** are both alike to You." Psalms 139:12

"Then God said, 'Let there be **light**'"; and there was **light**. And God saw the **light**, that it was good; and God divided the **light** from the darkness." Genesis 1:3

"Then God made two great **lights**: the greater **light** to rule the day, and the lesser **light** to rule the night. He made the stars also. God set them in the firmament of the heavens to give **light** on the earth, and to rule over the day and over the night, and to divide the **light** from the darkness. And God saw that it was good." Genesis 1:16-18

The Lord is the Light

"The Lord is my **light** and my salvation; Whom shall I fear?" Psalm 27:1

"For with You is the fountain of life; In Your **light** we see **light**." Psalms 36:9

"Then Jesus spoke to them again, saying, 'I am the **light** of the world. He who follows Me shall not walk in darkness, but have the **light** of life.'" John 8:12

We are sons of the Light

"While you have the **light**, believe in the **light**, that you may become sons of **light**.'" John 12:36

But the Light will leave this earth

"Then a mighty angel took up a stone like a great millstone and threw it into the sea, saying, 'Thus with violence the great city Babylon shall be thrown down, and shall not be found anymore. The sound of harpists, musicians, flutists, and trumpeters shall not be heard in you anymore. And no craftsman of any craft shall be found in you anymore. And the sound of a millstone shall not be heard in you anymore. And the **light** of a lamp shall not shine in you anymore. And the voice of bridegroom and bride shall not be heard in you anymore. For your merchants were the great men of the earth, for by your sorcery all the nations were deceived. And in her was found the blood of prophets and saints, and of all who were slain on the earth.'" Revelation 18:21-24

And the Light will dwell amongst us... forever

"And there shall be no more curse, but the throne of God and of the Lamb shall be in it, and His servants shall serve Him. They shall see His face, and His name shall be on their foreheads. And there shall be no night there: They need no lamp nor **light** of the sun, for the Lord God gives them **light**. And they shall reign forever and ever." Revelation 22:3-5

God is Light

Allegory is beautiful but literalness is inspiring. For God the Father created light and darkness, but in the beginning neither existed. But the Father existed before light and darkness, and now He is both light and darkness. For He created the light out of darkness, and He did this for the benefit of mankind. (Genesis 1:3) For how can we see the light, unless we are in the darkness? But we do know this, it is the image of light which we see, but not the source of the light itself. ...lly we see the image of the object, which is a reflection ...the light itself. That is until the Light came in this world, for the Light became flesh, and the Light is Life. "I am the light of the world. He who follows Me shall not walk in darkness, but have the light of life." (John 8:12)

The allegory is this, that God has become both light and darkness, for He makes no distinction between the two. (Psalms 139:12) But the good of its difference was meant for mankind. And on the first day He created the light, but darkness was made, for only in dark could we see the light. (Genesis 1:3) And on the second day He created the heavens, for the Light would dwell in the heavens. (Genesis 1:6-8) And on the third day He created the earth, but the earth would remain in the darkness. (Genesis 1:8-15) And on the fourth day He created two lights, the sun and the moon, so that all could see His creation on earth.(Genesis 1:16-18) And the earth had light but did not have God, for all we could see was the image of God.

The Son came to earth to give sight to mankind, for He is the Light of the world. (John 8:12) And through the Son we have no fear (Psalm 27:1) because His Word of Light is Life. (Psalms 36:9) The allegory is though we see the Light, we have just a glimpse of who our God is. For the spectrum of light that our eyes can see, is just one percent of the spectrum of light. And although we know the qualities of light, for now we know that it is wave (i.e. Einstein's theory of relativity) and particle (i.e. quantum theory of light), there are still qualities we don't understand. For Christ the Light came down to earth, so we could be with the Father. The blessing is that by knowing the Father, now we are called the sons of the Light. (John 12:36)

And the literalness of light is this, we no longer see the image of the light, for now we see that Christ is the Light. And what is the property of light? And if we take the theory of relativity, we can apply that which we know:

$$E = mc^2$$

E = energy m = mass

$$c = \text{speed of light} = 299{,}796 \text{ km/s}$$

And from this formula, if we assume the speed of light is constant, we can extrapolate that energy (albeit a very prodigious number) is proportional to mass.

Energy α *mass*

And as we know, the Father is energy and His creation is mass. Now we can see that the Father is all powerful, for He holds the creative and destructive force of His creation. *Yes, the destructive force of man.*

Father α *His creation*

For by the "wisdom" of man and relativity, we understand the destructive force of man. For through the destructive force of mankind, the earth and mankind shall perish. For when the nuclear holocaust ensues, a nuclear winter will follow, and the light of the sun will depart from the earth. "Then the fifth angel poured out his bowl on the throne of the beast, and his kingdom became full of darkness; and they gnawed their tongues because of the pain." (Revelation 16:10) And when the final trumpet sounds, Christ the Lamb and the Light of the world, the SON shall depart from the earth. And "the light of a lamp shall not shine in you anymore". (Revelation 18:21-24)

But by the love and mercy of God, after all our sins are reconciled, the heavens and earth will be destroyed, and all shall enter His kingdom. And man will understand the Light, for they will see the Light, for the Light of God will dwell amongst them... for the Light of our Life is God   "And there shall be no night there: They need no lamp nor light of the sun, for the Lord God gives them light. And

V I

Jesus is Sacrificial Blood (NKJV)
To Andrew the Prophet
Completed September 7, 2007

"For this is My **blood** of the new covenant, which is shed for many for the remission of sins. But I say to you, I will not drink of this fruit of the vine from now on until that day when I drink it new with you in My Father's kingdom." Matthew 26:28-29

The blood of the lamb was a sign of the covenant

"But you shall not eat flesh with its life, that is, its **blood**. Surely for your **lifeblood** I will demand a reckoning; from the hand of every beast I will require it, and from the hand of man. From the hand of every man's brother I will require the life of man. Whoever sheds man's **blood**, by man his **blood** shall be shed; for in the image of God He made man." Genesis 9:4

"Now the **blood** shall be a sign for you on the houses where you are. And when I see the **blood**, I will pass over you; and the plague shall not be on you to destroy you when I strike the land of Egypt..."For the Lord will pass through to strike the Egyptians; and when He sees the **blood** on the lintel and on the two doorposts, the Lord will pass over the door and not allow the destroyer to come into your houses to strike you." Exodus 12:13,23

"And Moses took the **blood**, sprinkled it on the people, and said, "Behold, the **blood** of the covenant which the Lord has made with you according to all these words.'"" Exodus 24:7

Due to their iniquity, God despised Israel's sacrifice

"To what purpose is the multitude of your sacrifices to Me?" says the Lord. 'I have had enough of burnt offerings of rams and the fat of fed cattle. I do not delight in the **blood** of bulls, or of lambs or goats.'" Isaiah 1:11

"For behold, the Lord comes out of His place to punish the inhabitants of the earth for their iniquity; the earth will also disclose her **blood**, and will no more cover her slain." Isaiah 26:21

"I will feed those who oppress you with their own flesh, and they shall be drunk with their own **blood** as with sweet wine. All flesh shall know that I, the Lord, am your Savior, and your Redeemer, the Mighty One of Jacob." Isaiah 49:26

"Why is Your apparel red, and Your garments like one who treads in the winepress? I have trodden the winepress alone, and from the peoples no one was with Me. For I have trodden them in My anger, and trampled them in My fury; their **blood** is sprinkled upon My garments, and I have stained all My robes. For the day of vengeance is in My heart, and the year of My redeemed has come." Isaiah 63:2-4

Christ the Lamb offered His blood for mankind

"For this is My **blood** of the new covenant, which is shed for many for the remission of sins. But I say to you, I will not drink of this fruit of the vine from now on until that day when I drink it new with you in My Father's kingdom." Matthew 26:28-29

"and you drank wine, the **blood** of the grapes." Deuteronomy 32:14

Christ the Lion will drink the blood of mankind

"Then Jesus said to them, 'Most assuredly, I say to you, unless you eat the flesh of the Son of Man and drink His **blood**, you have no life in you. Whoever eats My flesh and drinks My **blood** has eternal life, and I will raise him up at the last day. For My flesh is food

"And they cried with a loud voice, saying, 'How long, O Lord, holy and true, until You judge and avenge our **blood** on those who dwell on the earth?'" Revelation 6:10

"So the angel thrust his sickle into the earth and gathered the vine of the earth, and threw it into the great winepress of the wrath of God. And the winepress was trampled outside the city, and **blood** came out of the winepress, up to the horses' bridles, for one thousand six hundred furlongs" Revelation 14:19-20

Mankind's Blood Will Be Shed

Blood is the sustenance of life. And blood is the life of a man (Genesis 9:4), as God is the life of man's soul. And blood is the symbol of life, for it gives us a semblance of the kingdom to come. And blood is made of water and cells, that is moved by a pumping heart and carries oxygen throughout the body. And spiritual blood is sustained by the Father (water) and the sacrifice of Christ's blood (red cells), which is moved by the Spirit (heart), and carries life (oxygen) throughout the Church.

The Lord instructed His people, not to eat the blood of their food, for blood is the symbol of life. "But you shall not eat flesh with its life, that is, its blood."(Genesis 9:4) The Lord instructed His people to use the blood of the lamb, as His lasting promise to them. For the blood was the sign of life, that they would be His chosen people, if they would follow His commands. For on the eve they crossed the sea, the Israelites spread the blood of a lamb on the lintel and posts of two doors, that the angel of death would pass over them. (Exodus 12:13,23) And when His people were set free, the blood was sprinkled on them as a blessing. "Behold, the blood of the covenant which the Lord has made with you according to all these words."(Exodus 24:7)

But with greed and hate in their hearts, they would shed the blood of their foes. For they did not heed His command, but shed their enemies blood on the land, on land that was not theirs to keep. And covetous murder prevailed, and the Lord rebuked them in anger, "I have had enough of burnt offerings of rams and the fat of fed cattle. I do not delight in the blood of bulls, or of lambs or goats."(Isaiah 1:11) And by the words of the prophet, He promised man's blood would be shed, "For behold, the Lord comes out of His place to punish the inhabitants of the earth for their iniquity; the earth will also disclose her blood, and will no more cover her slain."(Isaiah 26:21) And He promised man's blood would be drunken like wine, "they shall be drunk with their own blood as with sweet wine."(Isaiah 49:26) For the wine would not come from the vine, but would come from the blood of mankind. "I have trodden the winepress alone."(Isaiah 63:2-4)

God sent His only begotten Son, that He would shed His blood for man. He humbled Himself and became a man, that through His Word and sacrifice, we would know the Way the Truth and Life. (John 14:6) And through the Son of Man's own will, He offered His blood for our sins. He was nailed to the cross and crucified, that our sins would be washed away. And on the third day He rose again, that the Spirit could dwell amongst us. "For this is My blood of the new covenant, which is shed for many for the remission of sins."(Matthew 26:28-29)

But few have shed their blood for the Lord, as He has shed His blood for mankind. For only the prophets, martyrs and saints, (the 144,000) have shed their own blood for His cause. And they will be pardoned from the wrath, for as the prophecy says, "he who overcomes shall not be hurt by the second death." (Revelation 2:11)

And the second death will come soon. For did He not promise to us, when at the table of sacrifice, and offered the cup of His blood?, "I will not drink of this fruit of the vine from now on until that day when I drink it new with you in My Father's kingdom." (Matthew 26:28-29) And what is the fruit of the vine? GRAPES. And what do we get from the grapes? WINE. And what does the wine represent? BLOOD. Yes and the metaphor is this, for "you drank wine, the ……"(Deuteronomy 32:14)

And the end times are upon us, for the day of judgment is near, and the prophecy shall be fulfilled. "So the angel thrust his sickle into the earth and gathered the vine of the earth, and threw it into the great winepress of the wrath of God. And the winepress was trampled outside the city, and blood came out of the winepress, up to the horses' bridles, for one thousand six hundred furlongs."(Revelation 14:19-20) Because mankind has turned from the Lord, and broken the covenant of His Son, **just as we drank the blood of the Lord, so shall He drink the blood of mankind**! And we can make peace with the Father, only through the payment of our sins. For the payment of our sins is this, that our sins must be paid by the blood of our death, and the death of this world and mankind. But remember that His judgment is fair, "for You shall judge the people righteously, And govern the nations on earth."(Psalms 67:4) And His love is everlasting, for through His payment and His justice, and through the winepress and the wrath, we can now return to the Father.

So let His wrath come, not with curse nor disdain, but with praise and thanksgiving, for He is just and true, and forgiving and faithful to us all. Let us fall to our knees and worship the King. He is King of all Kings and Lord of all Lords. COME LORD JESUS, COME!

VII

"The axe is already laid at the root of the trees; therefore every tree that does not bear good fruit is cut down and thrown into the **fire**." Matthew 3:10

Fire is Light: guidance in darkness

"The angel of the LORD appeared to him in a blazing fire from the midst of a bush; and he looked, and behold, the bush was burning with **fire**, yet the bush was not consumed." Exodus 3:3

"The LORD was going before them in a pillar of cloud by day to lead them on the way, and in a pillar of **fire** by night to give them light, that they might travel by day and by night." Exodus 13:21

"For throughout all their journeys, the cloud of the LORD was on the tabernacle by day, and there was **fire** in it by night, in the sight of all the house of Israel." Exodus 40:38

"Out of the heavens He let you hear His voice to discipline you; and on earth He let you see His great **fire**, and you heard His words from the midst of the **fire**" Deuteronomy 4:36

Fire is Heat: comfort in hardship

"For thus the LORD has told me, "I will look from My dwelling place quietly Like dazzling **heat** in the sunshine, Like a cloud of dew in the **heat** of harvest." Isaiah 18:4

coming out of his chamber; It rejoices

the heavens, And its circuit to the other end of them; And there is nothing hidden from its **heat**." Psalms 19:5-6

Fire is a Flame: the heart of the Holy Spirit

"He will baptize you with the Holy Spirit and **fire**." Matthew 3:11

"When the day of Pentecost had come, they were all together in one place. And suddenly there came from heaven a noise like a violent rushing wind, and it filled the whole house where they were sitting. And there appeared to them tongues as of **fire** distributing themselves, and they rested on each one of them." Acts 2:1-2

Fire is a Refiner: purifier of His chosen ones

"For He is like a refiner's **fire** and like fullers' soap.He will sit as a smelter and purifier of silver, and He will purify the sons of Levi and refine them like gold and silver, so that they may present to the LORD offerings in righteousness." Malachi 3:2

"And I will bring the third part through the **fire**, Refine them as silver is refined, And test them as gold is tested. They will call on My name, And I will answer them; I will say, 'They are My people,' And they will say, 'The LORD is my God.'" Zechariah 13:9

And then, the judgment by fire arrives

"For the day will show it because it is to be revealed with **fire**, and the **fire** itself will test the quality of each man's work." 1 Corinthians 3:13

"Then the LORD rained on Sodom and Gomorrah brimstone and **fire** from the LORD out of heaven" Genesis 19:24

"For behold, the LORD will come in **fire** And His chariots like the whirlwind, To render His anger with fury, And His rebuke with flames of **fire**. For the LORD will execute judgment by **fire** And by His sword on all flesh, And those slain by the LORD will be many." Isaiah 66:15-16

"So it will be at the end of the age; the angels will come forth and take out the wicked from among the righteous, and will throw them into the furnace of **fire**; in that place there will be weeping and gnashing of teeth." Matthew 13:49

And the judgment by fire is GREAT

"Then the angel took the censer and filled it with the **fire** of the altar, and threw it to the earth; and there followed peals of thunder and sounds and flashes of lightning and an earthquake. And the seven angels who had the seven trumpets prepared themselves to sound them. The first sounded, and there came hail and **fire**, mixed with blood, and they were thrown to the earth; and a third of the earth was burned up, and a third of the trees were burned up, and all the green grass was burned up. The second angel sounded, and {something} like a great mountain burning with **fire** was thrown into the sea; and a third of the sea became blood. The third angel sounded, and a great star fell from heaven, burning like a torch, and it fell on a third of the rivers and on the springs of waters.... A third of mankind was killed by these three plagues, by the **fire** and the smoke and the brimstone which proceeded out of their mouths.." Revelation 8-9

"And I saw something like a sea of glass mixed with **fire**" Revelation 15:2

"The fourth angel poured out his bowl upon the sun, and it was given to it to scorch men with **fire**." Revelation 16:8

But He is Faithful and True to all men

"And I saw heaven opened, and behold, a white horse, and He who sat on it is called Faithful and True, and in righteousness He judges and wages war. His eyes are a flame of **fire**, and on His head are many diadems; and He has a name written on Him which no one knows except Himself. He is clothed with a robe dipped in blood, and His name is called The Word of God." Revelation 19:11-12

Fire Refines and Fire Burns

His anger was kindled at the cross, and now has been set all aflame, for the Lamb that died has become the Lion. Christ the Son has the nature of two, for by His love He saves mankind, and by His wrath He will destroy mankind. For as was promised, He came to save men as the Lamb, but returns to judge as the Lion. "Stop weeping; behold, the Lion that is from the tribe of Judah, the Root of David, has overcome so as to open the book and its seven seals." (Revelation 5:5)

Likewise fire has the nature of two, for it once was used to help mankind, but now will be used to destroy mankind. And what is a fire? A fire is a chemical reaction, that releases both light and heat, and appears as a flame.

What does the light of a fire do? It guides mankind in the darkness. And the Father appeared to Moses, as a bush of fire on the mountain. (Exodus 3:3) And as the Lord led His people, He appeared as a pillar of fire (the "shekhinah"), so that they could travel by night. (Exodus 13:21) And He dwelt with them in His temple (Exodus 40:38), and they heard His Words from the fire. (Deuteronomy 4:36) But the true light was given to men, through His Son the true Word of God. For Christ is the Light of the world, He was sent down to earth by the Father, to lead the world out of the darkness. "Then Jesus again spoke to them, saying, 'I am the Light of the world; he who follows Me will not walk in the darkness, but will have the Light of life.'" (John 8:12)

What does the heat of a fire do? Heat of a fire brings comfort, to those who've been out in the cold. For even now He is waiting, for us to return to His place, "quietly like dazzling heat in the sunshine." (Isaiah 18:4) For Christ the Groom will return, to comfort those who are faithful. For He "is as a bridegroom coming out of his chamber; rejoices as a strong man to run his course. Its rising is from one end of the heavens, and its circuit to the other end of them; and there is nothing hidden from its heat." (Psalms 19:5-6)

And what do flames represent? They represent the heart and the fruits of the Spirit. For the Holy Spirit sets us aflame, to do His good works, to produce His fruits, and to strengthen His kingdom. For the Holy Spirit was given to us, through the sacrifice of Christ's blood, and the payment by death on the cross. (Matthew 3:11) For as it is said, when the Spirit came down on the disciples, the Spirit "appeared to them tongues as of fire distributing themselves, and they rested on each one of them." (Acts 2:1-2) For it is through the Holy Spirit, that our hearts are emptied and filled, and are made complete through the Son, so that we can be sons of the Father.

And what else does fire do? It purifies metal into fine silver and gold. Just as a fire removes impurities from metal, so does the Lord remove the sins of His servants, and purifies them into righteous servants of gold and silver. (Malachi 3:2). For He strips them of their earthly clothes, and gives them robes of sacrifice, righteousness, holiness, and love. For when they are raised, the world will then see, that "these are the ones who come out of the great tribulation, and they have washed their robes and made them white in the blood of the Lamb. For this reason, "they are before the throne of God; and they serve Him day and night in His temple; and He who sits on the throne will spread His tabernacle over them." (Revelation 7:14-15) For they will be called His people, and they will proclaim "The LORD is my God." (Zechariah 13:9).

But woe to those whose lamps are not lit, for His fire does not give light nor comfort, but shall judge the work of men rightfully. For as was foretold, each man will be judged by his works. "For the day will show it because it is to be revealed with fire, and the fire itself will test the quality of each man's work." (1 Corinthians 3:13)

The Lord gave us warning of the day that would come, when He judged the two cities (Sodom and Gomorrah) with fire. (Genesis 19:24) And the Lord gave us warning through the prophets of old, that He would return before the fire. (Isaiah 66:15-16) For did He not warn when He walked on this earth, that the furnace of fire
? (Matthew 13:49) Ah, but so few have heeded His

Be prepared. And know that the judgment by fire will be horrifying indeed. And the prophecy words will hold true, for the trumpets will sound of the news, that will warn the earth of the fire to come. (Rev 8 and 9). And do you recall how the martyrs were burned, how their suffering would last just a moment. But now the laws of death are withheld, and many will burn for five fateful months. For they will beg and plead for their death, but death will be withheld until all has been paid.

"But to torment for five months; and their torment was like the torment of a scorpion when it stings a man. And in those days men will seek death and will not find it; they will long to die, and death flees from them." Revelation 9:5

And what is the cause of the fire? Yes none other than man himself. For the nuclear age began in Hiroshima, on August 6, 1945.

"Then the time will come when men will curse the names of Los Alamos and Hiroshima. The people of this world must unite or they will perish." Robert Oppenheimer, director of the Manhattan Project and the Trinity atomic bomb project.

Hiroshima – August 6, 1945

And read the words of a survivor from Hiroshima, "In the early stages, the only treatment I received from my burns was the application of a mixture of ash and oil as a substitute from medicine. I do not know how many times I yelled 'kill me!' because of the severe pain and desperate feeling."

And for the wretched souls that survive past the first three bowls of wrath, the ozone layer will burn away, the earth will become a fiery inferno, and the UV rays will burn them alive. (Revelation 16:8)

But He is a forgiving God. And after all the debts are paid, Christ the One who is Faithful and True, will destroy Satan and his rule over earth, and death and suffering will be no more. (Revelation 19:11-12). For even when the chaff is burned, ashes remain; and even those who deserve no mercy, they will be saved. "If any man's work is burned up, he will suffer loss; but he himself will be saved, yet so as through fire." 1 Corinthians 3:16

So make haste to turn to the Lamb, that your works through the Spirit hold true, that your judgment may be merciful ... for all must go through the fire of judgment, the righteous fire of Truth.

"The angel of the LORD appeared to him in a blazing fire from the midst of a bush; And he looked, and behold, the bush was burning with fire, yet the bush was not consumed." Exodus 3:3

As the LORD appeared to Moses as the burning bush on Mount Sinai which was not consumed, a burning bush shall return, but this Bush shall be consumed by the Fire.

VIII

God is Sacrificial Love (NKJV)
To Andrew the Prophet
Completed September 19, 2007

"For God so **loved** the world, that He gave His only begotten Son, that whoever believes in Him shall not perish, but have eternal life." John 3:16

Rule of Love #1: LOVE GOD FIRST

"You shall **love** the Lord your God with all your heart, with all your soul, and with all your might." Deuteronomy 6:5

"And He said to him, 'YOU SHALL **LOVE** THE LORD YOUR GOD WITH ALL YOUR HEART, AND WITH ALL YOUR SOUL, AND WITH ALL YOUR MIND.' This is the great and foremost commandment." Matthew 22:37-38

Rule of Love #2: LOVE OTHERS

"You shall not take vengeance, nor bear any grudge against the children of your people, but you shall **love** your neighbor as yourself: I am the Lord." Leviticus 19:18

"The second is like it, 'YOU SHALL **LOVE** YOUR NEIGHBOR AS YOURSELF.' On these two commandments depend the whole Law and the Prophets." Matthew 22:39

"But I say to you, **love** your enemies and pray for those who persecute you" Matthew 5:44

Consequence #1: LACK OF LOVE WILL BE PUNISHED

will set them ablaze," says the LORD of hosts, 'so that it will leave them neither root nor branch ... You will tread down the wicked, for they will be ashes under the soles of your feet on the day which I am preparing,' says the LORD of hosts." Malachi 4:1-3

Consequence #2 GODLY LOVE WILL BE REWARDED

"He who has My commandments and keeps them is the one who **loves** Me; and he who **loves** Me will be **loved** by My Father, and I will **love** him and will disclose Myself to him." John 14:21

"But (God) chose the tribe of Judah, Mount Zion which He **loved**." Psalms 78:68

"The Lord **loves** the gates of Zion More than all the dwellings of Jacob." Psalms 87:2

"Greater **love** has no one than this, that one lay down his life for his friends." John 15:13

"**Love** is patient, **love** is kind and is not jealous; **love** does not brag and is not arrogant, does not act unbecomingly; it does not seek its own, is not provoked, does not take into account a wrong suffered, does not rejoice in unrighteousness, but rejoices with the truth; bears all things, believes all things, hopes all things, endures all things. **Love** never fails." 1 Corinthians 13:4-8

Love Never Fails

What is love? Love is God and God is love. For love originates from God, is sustained by God, and completes all things through God. And we did not love God first, but it is God who loved us first. And God is not a jealous God, for the love we bestow on Him originates and emanates from Himself. But there is one thing that we do comprehend, that we cannot understand the full depth of His love, for it is ubiquitous, infinite, eternal and true. And who can understand, the scope of His love, that is higher than the clouds, and louder than the thunder? (Job 36:29) For who else would sacrifice, His only begotten Son for the sake of mankind? (John 3:16)

His first commandment is this, that we should love the Lord our God with all our heart, with all our soul, and with all our mind. He gave this command to His people, when they walked across the Red Sea. (Deuteronomy 6:5) And again He taught this to His disciples, when they walked with His only Son (Matthew 22:37). But what does this mean? For to love with our "all" is impossible in our fallen state as earthly beings. But to love with our "all" will be possible in our risen state as heavenly beings. And to love with all your hearts is to love with all your spirit, for the heart and the spirit are one and the same. For through the Holy Spirit, the heart strengthens our faith in God, and gives us the gifts to produce His fruits. And to love with all your soul, means to love in the hope and the sustenance of the Father. For all our souls come from the Father, and live in the hope of returning to Him. And to love with all our mind means to love with the mind of Christ. For the mind of Christ is the Truth, and the Truth of God is His Word; "and the Word became flesh and dwelt among us". (John 1:14) Thus the heart yields the faith and the fruits of the Spirit, and the soul yields the hope and the sustenance of the Father, and the mind yields the Word and the love of the Son.

His second commandment is this, to love our neighbors as ourselves. (Leviticus 19:18, Matthew 22:39) For as we are children of God, we are commanded to love not just our neighbors, but also to love all strangers, and yes we are even to love our enemies. (Matthew 5:44) For who are we to say whom God loves, for in truth the Lord loves all men. For we all come from one Father; and as He did promise to us, "the Lord shall be King over all the earth. In that day it shall be 'the Lord is one', and His name one"(Zechariah 14:9) For all shall be brothers and sisters in Christ, and all shall love one another as He has loved us. So let us not seek the vengeance of God, for the Lion will judge all men with the Truth. "For He is coming, for He is coming to judge the earth. He shall judge the world with righteousness, and the peoples with His truth." (Psalms 96:13)

And the first consequence of love is this, all wrongs in the world must be righted. For the Father is perfect, and all wrongs must be righted, before man can return to the Father. For as it was said, "'You will tread down the wicked, for they will be ashes under the soles of your feet on the day which I am preparing,' says the LORD of hosts." (Malachi 4:3) For all have heard His Word of Truth, but many have refused to follow Him; and yet others have persecuted our Lord and His people. But now all mankind shall be paid for their deeds, "for you shall not depart from there till you have paid the very last mite." (Luke 12:59) So do not have vengeance for those who have harmed you, for they shall receive their just due. And pray for forgiveness from those you have harmed, for you too shall receive your just due.

The second consequence of love is this, that God will reward those who love Him, for He loves those who love His commands. There is a hierarchy to those who have loved Him, "for to everyone who has, more will be given, and he will have abundance; but from him who does not have, even what he has will be taken away." (Matthew 25:29) For those who have faithfully followed Him, and to those who have obeyed His commands, He will grant great rewards on that day, for He will disclose their names to the Father. (John 14:21) And they will be called "sons of the Most High". (Luke 6:35)

And to those who have sacrificed their lives for His sake, He has granted immeasurable rewards. For these are the prophets, and martyrs, and saints, who have sacrificed their lives for His sake (the 144,000). For they are His firstfruits as He did say, "but many who are first will be last, and the last first." (Matthew 19:30) And turn over **144** for they are **(hh1)** His holy ones. For they are also the tribe of Judah and Mount Zion (Psalms 78:68). And turn over ZION for they are the NO12, "the number of those who were sealed". For the 144,000 are the 12 tribes of 12 thousand. (Revelation 7:4) And the kings of the 144,000 are the 12 saints who guard the 12 gates. (Psalms 87:2) For these are the 12 apostles of Christ, who will guard the 12 gates of Jerusalem. (Revelation 21:21) And as He has promised, "Truly I say to you, that you who have followed Me, in the regeneration when the Son of Man will sit on His glorious throne, you also shall sit upon 12 thrones, judging the 12 tribes of Israel." (Matthew 19:28)

But the greatest One of all is the throne of the King, for He will Lord over all of the nations. (Revelation 15:4) "But there is no greater love than this, that one lay down his life for his friends." (John 15:13) For who is the greatest love of all, but Christ the Lamb, for He laid down His life for mankind. And the least of His disciples hopes to follow in His footsteps.

Love can be summarized in the following way. If we take what we know which is true, God is Love, and apply it to the letter of God's love, then we finally understand who our God is:

God

is patient

God is kind God is

not jealous God

does not   brag

God   is not   arrogant

God does not act unbecomingly

God does not seek His own, is not provoked

God does not take into account a wrong suffered

God does not rejoice in unrighteousness, but rejoices with the truth

God bears all things, believes all things, hopes all things, endures all things.

GOD NEVER FAILS.

(1 Corinthians 13:4-8)

"And in as much as they gave the command to leave the stump and roots of the tree, your kingdom shall be assured to you, after you come to know that Heaven rules." (Daniel 4:26)

I X

We are His Harvest (NKJV) To
Andrew the Prophet Completed
September 25, 2007

"Thrust in Your sickle and reap, for the time has come for You to reap, for the **harvest** of the earth is ripe." Revelation 14:15

The Sower is Christ

"He who **sows** the good seed is the Son of Man." Matthew 13:37

The Seed is the Word of God and His childrem

"Now the parable is this: The **seed** is the word of God" Luke 8:11

"The field is the world, the good **seeds** are the sons of the kingdom" Matthew 13:37

The Father is Water

"'Let the **waters** abound with an abundance of living creatures, and let birds fly above the earth across the face of the firmament of the heavens.' So God created great sea creatures and every living thing that moves, with which the **waters** abounded, according to their kind, and every winged bird according to its kind. And God saw that it was good." Genesis 1:20-21

"Most assuredly, I say to you, unless one is born of **water** and the Spirit, he cannot enter the kingdom of God." John 3:5

The Son is Light

"Then Jesus spoke to them again, saying, 'I am the **light** of the world. He who follows Me shall not walk in darkness, but have the **light** of life.'" John 8:12

"And as they were eating, Jesus took bread, blessed it and broke it, and gave it to them and said, 'Take, eat; this is My body.' Then He took the cup, and when He had given thanks He gave it to them, and they all drank from it. And He said to them, 'This is My blood of the new covenant, which is shed for many.'" Mark 14:22-23

The Holy Spirit is the Breath of Life

"The Spirit of God has made me, and the **breath** of the Almighty gives me life" Job 33:4

"Then Jesus said to them again, 'Peace to you! As the Father has sent Me, I also send you.' And when He had said this, He **breathed** on them, and said to them, 'Receive the Holy Spirit.'"
John 20:21-22.

The harvest is the fruits of the Spirit

"Thrust in Your sickle and reap, for the time has come for You to reap, for the **harvest** of the earth is ripe." Revelation 14:15

"Until the Spirit is poured upon us from on high, and the wilderness becomes a **fruitful** field, and the **fruitful** field is counted as a forest." Isaiah 32:15

"These are the ones who were not defiled with women, for they are virgins. These are the ones who follow the Lamb wherever He goes. These were redeemed from among men, being **firstfruits** to God and to the Lamb." Revelation 14:4

"we also who have the **firstfruits** of the Spirit, even we ourselves groan within ourselves, eagerly waiting for the adoption, the redemption of our body." Romans 8:23

We will be judged by our work, the fruits of the Spirit

"For no other foundation can anyone lay than that which is laid, which is Jesus Christ. Now if anyone builds on this foundation with gold, silver, precious stones, wood, hay, straw, each one's **work** will become manifest; for the Day will declare it, because it will be revealed by fire; and the fire will test each one's **work**, of what sort it is. If anyone's **work** which he has built on it endures, he will receive a reward. If anyone's **work** is burned, he will suffer loss; but he himself will be saved, yet so as through fire." 1 Corinthians 3:11-15.

We are His Harvest, the Fruits of the Spirit

We are the harvest of His sowing. For the seed of the harvest has been sown, and the sower is our Lord Jesus Christ. (Matthew 13:37). For the seed is the Word, and the Word was made flesh. (Luke 8:11) And the Word dwelt with man, that the seed of His children could be sown. (Matthew 13:37) And the time is now near, for the beast has arrived, and the seal has been broken, and the harvest is ripe.

What is required for a good harvest? A harvest requires three elements to survive. And these elements are water, sunlight, and oxygen; for without these three the harvest would perish. And any child of Christ requires three elements, in order to live in this world. And the first element is water, the sustenance of life with the Father. The second element is sunlight, the Light and the Son of God. And the third element is air, the breath of life and the Spirit. For without these Three, the harvest of His children would perish. "For there are three that bear witness in heaven: the Father, the Word, and the Holy Spirit; and these three are one." (1 John 5:7)

And what is water? Water is a fundamental molecule, that is required for life to exist, for water is the building block of life. Even scientists with their atheistic ideals, say water is needed for any organism to survive. And when God created the earth, He created the water to give life, that it may "abound with an abundance of living creatures". (Genesis 1:20-21.) And just as the creatures of the earth, require

.. .. of Christ depends on the Father to

And why is sunlight necessary? Photosynthesis is a basic process in biology, that harvests the energy of the sunlight, and converts sunlight's energy into food. The source of that sunlight is the sun. As children of Christ we require the Light, and the source of Light is from the Son. (John 8:12), For He is the sun that gives us the Light, in this dark and desolate world. The Light that He gives is His body and His blood (Mark 14:22-23). And His body is the bread of life, the Word that feeds His children. And His blood is His sacrifice for man, and through His death the Spirit gives us breath.

And what is air? Air is composed of CO2, a molecule that couples with photosynthesis, and converts sunlight into fuel. Thus plants can convert sunlight, water, and air into fuel. We can write the reaction of the process as::

$$6\,H_2O + 6\,CO_2 + sunlight \Rightarrow C_6H_{12}O_6 + 6\,O_2$$

Thus

6 water + 6 carbon dioxide + sunlight ⇒ 1 sugar + 6 oxygen

The "Spirit of God has made us", and the "breath of the Almighty gives us life". (Job 33:4) For when Christ arose on the third day, He returned to breathe the Spirit into us. (John 20:21-22) For the life that we breathe is the Spirit, and through the Spirit we produce His fruits. For the breath of the Spirit, works with the Father and the Son, that we may produce His fruits. And from the last equation, the overall reaction is:

Father + Holy Spirit + Son ⇒ Fruits + Holy Spirit

Thus

The Holy Trinity ⇒ Fruits through the Holy Spirit

Thus, the "harvest of the earth" (Revelations 14:15) are the fruits of the Holy Spirit. (Isaiah 32:15) And the fruits of the Holy Spirit are produced by the sustenance in the Father, by the blood and Word of Christ, and by the breath of the Holy Spirit. And His firstfruits will be harvested (the 144,000), for "these were redeemed from among men, being firstfruits to God and to the Lamb." (Revelation 14:4) For His firstfruits have awaited this day, "eagerly waiting for the adoption, the redemption of our body." (Romans 8:23)

The time is near and His promises are true, for each one must go through the fire. And know that the only true rock is our Lord. "For no other foundation can anyone lay than that which is laid, which is Jesus Christ. Now if anyone builds on this foundation with gold, silver, precious stones, wood, hay, straw, each one's work will become manifest; for the Day will declare it, because it will be revealed by fire; and the fire will test each one's work, of what sort it is. If anyone's work which he has built on it endures, he will receive a reward. If anyone's work is burned, he will suffer loss; but he himself will be saved, yet so as through fire." (1 Corinthians 3:11-15) The Lord does not return as the sower, for the Lord will return as the reaper. The Lord does not return as the Lamb, for the Lord will return as the Lion. So make haste and complete His good works, for the fire will come, and each will be measured by his fruit. The bowls of wrath loom, the Judgment draws near, for the "harvest of the earth is ripe." (Revelation 14:15)

BIOSYNTHESIS AND HIS HARVEST

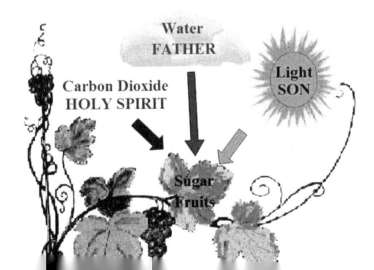

X

Christ is the Sower, We are the Seed (NASB)
To Andrew the Prophet
Completed September 26, 2007

"He who **sows** the good **seed** is the Son of Man. The field is the world, the good **seeds** are the sons of the kingdom, but the tares are the sons of the wicked one. The enemy who sowed them is the devil, the harvest is the end of the age, and the reapers are the angels. Therefore as the tares are gathered and burned in the fire, so it will be at the end of this age." Matthew 13:37-38

God first created the seed to propagate the earth

"Then God said, 'Let the earth sprout vegetation, plants yielding **seed**, and fruit trees on the earth bearing fruit after their kind with **seed** in them'; and it was so. The earth brought forth vegetation, plants yielding **seed** after their kind, and trees bearing fruit with **seed** in them, after their kind; and God saw that it was good." Genesis 1:11-12

The first seeds of mankind were fallen

"And I will put enmity Between you and the woman, And between your **seed** and her **seed**; He shall bruise you on the head, And you shall bruise him on the heel." Genesis 3:15

"Then the angel of the LORD called to Abraham a second time from heaven, and said, 'By Myself I have sworn, declares the LORD, because you have done this thing and have not withheld your son, your only son, indeed I will greatly bless you, and I will greatly multiply your **seed** as the stars of the heavens and as the sand which is on the seashore; and your **seed** shall possess the gate of their enemies. In your **seed** all the nations of the earth shall be blessed, because you have obeyed My voice.'" Genesis 22:15-18

"Thus all the tithe of the land, of the **seed** of the land or of the fruit of the tree, is the LORD'S; it is holy to the LORD." Leviticus 27:30

"The Lord has removed men far away, and the forsaken places are many in the midst of the land. But yet a tenth will be in it, and will return and be for consuming, as a terebinth tree or as an oak, whose stump remains when it is cut down. So the holy **seed** shall be its stump.'" Isaiah 6:12-13

Christ sows the righteous seed

"Now to Abraham and his **Seed** were the promises made. He does not say, 'And to seeds,' as of many, but as of one, 'And to your **Seed**,' who is Christ." Galatians 3:16

"And when He had removed him, He raised up for them David as king, to whom also He gave testimony and said, 'I have found David the son of Jesse, a man after My own heart, who will do all My will.' From this man's **seed**, according to the promise, God raised up for Israel a Savior Jesus" Acts 13:22-23

"The **seed** is the word of God" Luke 8:11

"Whoever has been born of God does not sin, for His **seed** remains in him; and he cannot sin, because he has been born of God." 1 John 3:9

We each bear fruit at God's preordained time

"Then He will give the rain for your **seed** with which you sow the ground." Isaiah 30:23

"I am the Lord, and there is no other. I have not spoken in secret, in a dark place of the earth; I did not say to the **seed** of Jacob, 'Seek Me in vain'; I, the Lord, speak righteousness, I declare things that are right." Isaiah 45:18-19 was made; and it was appointed through angels by the hand of a mediator." Galatians 3:19

Our shells need to be broken before we can bear fruit

"Behold, a sower went out to sow. And as he sowed, some **seed** fell by the wayside; and the birds came and devoured them. Some fell on stony places, where they did not have much earth; and they immediately sprang up because they had no depth of earth. But when the sun was up they were scorched, and because they had no root they withered away. And some fell among thorns, and the thorns sprang up and choked them. But others fell on good ground and yielded a crop: some a hundredfold, some sixty, some thirty." Matthew 13:3-8

"Yet I had planted you a noble vine, a **seed** of highest quality. How then have you turned before Me into the degenerate plant of an alien vine?" Jeremiah 2:21

And as He promises, the rewards will be great

"I have made a covenant with My chosen; I have sworn to David My servant, I will establish your **seed** forever And build up your throne to all generations." Psalms 89:3-4

"For the **seed** shall be prosperous, the vine shall give its fruit, the ground shall give her increase, and the heavens shall give their dew. I will cause the remnant of this people to possess all these things." Zechariah 8:12

"The kingdom of heaven is like a mustard seed, which a man took and sowed in his field, which indeed is the least of all the **seeds**; but when it is grown it is greater than the herbs and becomes a tree, so that the birds of the air come and nest in its branches" Matthew 13:31-32

His children are His Seed

God created the earth. And when God created the earth, He created the vegetation. And with the vegetation, He created the seed that it may spread throughout the earth. And when it was complete, "God saw that it was good." (Genesis 1:11-12)

Who was the first seed? The first seed was of Adam and Eve. But like the fallen state of man, the first seed of man was fallen. For the perfect Seed is complete in itself, able to grow and bear fruit on its own. Unlike the perfect Seed of God, their seeds were not complete, but required their union to produce a child. "For this reason a man shall leave his father and his mother, and be joined to his wife; and they shall become one flesh." (Genesis 2:24) And as God promised, the seed of their union would be fraught with strife, "And I will put enmity between you and the woman, And between your seed and her seed; He shall bruise you on the head, And you shall bruise him on the heel." (Genesis 3:15) And with the fall of man, and the fallen state of their seed, came the fallen state of all men, for they were given to idolatry, adultery, covetousness, thievery, murder, and ultimately death.

But by God's grace, He made a covenant through Abraham, the father of the nations; for by his faith, God promised to spread his seed through the nations. (Genesis 22:15-18) And through His covenant, He commanded His people to remember Him, through the sacrifice from the seed of the land. (Leviticus 27:30). But they forgot His covenant, and transgressed His ways, and they were punished for their wicked ways. Yet He kept His promise that the holy seed would return, for "the holy seed shall be its stump.'" (Isaiah 6:12-13)

What are the characteristics of a seed? A seed contains an embryo and a food supply enclosed within a hard shell. A seed can remain dormant for thousands of years (in fact, the oldest viable seed is 2000 years old, a seed from Herod's courts), and it will not grow until it is germinated. The trigger for its germination is threefold: water, sunlight, and oxygen; but, the shell of the seed must be split,

The Structure of a Seed

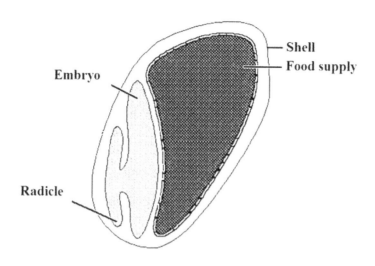

Because of the fallen state of man, a covenant was made with our forefathers, that from their seed a Savior would come (Galatians 3:16/Acts 13:22-23). And the Savior came to earth, to sow His holy Seed, for "He who sows a good seed is the Son of Man"(Matthew 13:37). For God descended to earth as a man, that we would know the Truth of God. And the Truth of God is the Word of God, and the Word of God is the holy Seed. (Luke 8:11). And through His death and resurrection, the children of God are now His seed, for "the good seeds are the sons of the kingdom." (Matthew 13:37). But unlike the seed of Adam and Eve, the Seed of the Savior is perfect and complete. And a true follower of Christ is a complete embryo, or child of God, and is no longer at enmity with the Father. For no longer are we born of man, but now we are born of God. And no longer does God see the sin of man, but now He sees the perfection of Christ, for the Seed of His Word lives in us. (1 John 3:9)

As a seed is released in a dormant state, with the proper condition grows and bears fruit, so too are we born dormant to God, but at God's preordained time and plan, grow as His children and bear fruits of the Spirit. The three elements needed to germinate the seed are water, sunlight, and oxygen. And the first element is water, the sustenance of life. Just as a seed needs water to grow, we need the sustenance of the Father to grow. (Isaiah 30:23) And sunlight triggers the seed to grow. And our sunlight is the Light of Christ, for just as a seed cannot grow in the darkness, neither can we grow without His Word. (Isaiah 45:18-19). And oxygen mediates the respiratory pathway, which produces energy from light. And the Holy Spirit "mediates" our lives, for through His gifts we produce His fruits. (Galatians 3:19) Thus all three, the Father, the Son, and the Holy Spirit, are needed for His children to grow and bear fruit.

Although Christ sows us with His Word, we still must take root in Him. The seed has a root called a radicle, which is the anchor of the seed in the earth. And we must take root in the Word of the Son, through the heart of the Spirit, and the sustenance of the Father. And just as the shell of the hardened seed, needs to be broken before it takes root, so does the shell of our hardened hearts, need to be broken to take root in Him. But many have fallen away, for many have had "no firm root in themselves, but are only temporary." (Mark 4:17) For many were like seeds on the wayside. They did not take root but were lured by temptations. And many were like seeds parched by the sun, though they took root, their roots were not strong, to withstand the persecution of men. Yet others were like seeds in the thorns, though they took root, the worries of the world choked them out. (Matthew 13:3-7) For they all have turned from the noble Vine (Jeremiah 2:21), for it is Christ who is the Root of Life. For it is Christ who is "the root and the descendant of David, the bright morning star." (Revelation 22:16)

But His children did take root in Christ. And they rejected the temptations of this world, and they endured the persecutions of this world, and they forsook the worries of this world. And now that the end is near, they are assured that their rewards will be great. (Matthew 13:8) For He "will establish your seed forever And build up your throne to all generations." (Psalms 89:3-4) And "the seed shall be prosperous, the vine shall give its fruit, the ground shall give her increase, and the heavens shall give their dew".(Zechariah there till you have paid the last penny." (Matthew 5:26). But after the last penny is paid, we can rest in hope and assurance. For the seed of the kingdom was created for all, for the kingdom has grown far and wide, and all shall rest in its branches. (Matthew 13:31-32)

X I

Christ is the Vine, We are the Branch (NASB)
To Andrew the Prophet
Completed September 28, 2007

"I am the true **vine**, and My Father is the **vinedresser**. Every branch in Me that does not bear fruit, He takes away; and every branch that bears fruit, He prunes it so that it may bear more fruit." John 15:1-2

The vine is as old as mankind

"Then Noah began farming and planted a **vineyard**" Genesis 9:20

"You shall not sow your **vineyard** with two kinds of seed, or all the produce of the seed which you have sown and the increase of the **vineyard** will become defiled." Deuteronomy 22:9

"When you gather the grapes of your **vineyard**, you shall not go over it again; it shall be for the alien, for the orphan, and for the widow." Deuteronomy 24:21

The vine of mankind failed

"Yet I planted you a choice **vine**, A completely faithful seed. How then have you turned yourself before Me Into the degenerate shoots of a foreign **vine**? Although you wash yourself with lye And use much soap, The stain of your iniquity is before Me" Jeremiah 2:21-22

"He dug it all around, removed its stones, And planted it with the choicest **vine**. And He built a tower in the middle of it And also hewed out a wine vat in it; Then He expected it to produce good grapes,

What more was there to do for My **vineyard** that I have not done in it? Why, when I expected it to produce good grapes did it produce worthless ones? So now let Me tell you what I am going to do to My **vineyard**: I will remove its hedge and it will be consumed; I will break down its wall and it will become trampled ground. I will lay it waste; It will not be pruned or hoed, But briars and thorns will come up. I will also charge the clouds to rain no rain on it." Isaiah 5:2-6

But the Lord is faithful to the vine

"You removed a **vine** from Egypt; You drove out the nations and planted it. You cleared the ground before it, And it took deep root and filled the land." Psalms 80:8

"And there He makes the hungry to dwell, So that they may establish an inhabited city, And sow fields and plant **vineyards**, And gather a fruitful harvest." Psalms 107:36-37

"Your wife shall be like a fruitful **vine** Within your house, Your children like olive plants Around your table. Behold, for thus shall the man be blessed Who fears the LORD." Psalms 128:3-4

Christ is the true Vine and the Father is the Vinedresser

"I am the true **vine**, and My Father is the **vinedresser**. Every branch in Me that does not bear fruit, He takes away; and every branch that bears fruit, He prunes it so that it may bear more fruit." John 15:1-2

"In that day, 'A **vineyard** of wine, sing of it! I, the LORD, am its keeper; I water it every moment. So that no one will damage it, I guard it night and day.'" Isaiah 27:2-3

We are the branches

"I am the vine, you are the **branches**; he who abides in Me and I in him, he bears much fruit, for apart from Me you can do nothing." John 15:5

"You will say then, "**Branches** were broken off so that I might be grafted in." Quite right, they were broken off for their unbelief, but you stand by your faith. Do not be conceited, but fear; for if God did not spare the natural **branches**, He will not spare you, either." Romans 11:19-20

"And they also, if they do not continue in their unbelief, will be grafted in, for God is able to graft them in again. For if you were cut off from what is by nature a wild olive tree, and were grafted contrary to nature into a cultivated olive tree, how much more will these who are the natural **branches** be grafted into their own olive tree?" Romans 11:23-24

But the branches will be burned, and the grapes crushed

"If anyone does not abide in Me, he is thrown away as a **branch** and dries up; and they gather them, and cast them into the fire and they are burned." John 15:6

"Then another angel, the one who has power over fire, came out from the altar; and he called with a loud voice to him who had the sharp sickle, saying, 'Put in your sharp sickle and gather the clusters from the **vine** of the earth, because her grapes are ripe.' So the angel swung his sickle to the earth and gathered the clusters from the **vine** of the earth, and threw them into the great wine press of the wrath of God. And the wine press was trodden outside the city, and blood came out from the wine press, up to the horses' bridles, for a distance of two hundred miles." Rev 14:18-20

Christ is the Vine, We are the Branch

The grapevine is one of the oldest cultivated plants in the world, for its wine is as old as the nations. The vine was first grown during Noah and the flood, for from it he planted the first vineyard. (Genesis 9:20) And His people were ordered not to mix other seeds, with the seeds of the vineyard, less the vineyard be defiled. (Deuteronomy 22:9) And He told them not to worship, other idols of the nations, less His people be defiled. They were told to leave a

But His people disobeyed His commands, and grafted themselves out of the vine. (Jeremiah 2:21-22)   Thus they were defiled, and their fruit had no worth. And the Lord would punish His people, for He removed their hedge, and trampled them down, and lay them waste, and they were consumed. (Isaiah 5:2-6).

But the Lord is a faithful God, who continues to give fruit of the vine.   Did He not deliver His people from Egypt, and establish a kingdom in their presence? (Psalms 80:8) And does He not deliver the homeless and hungry, and give them shelter and food? (Psalms 107:36-37)   And does He not give us our children, the fruit of the womb of our seed? (Psalms 128:3-4) And in kindness and mercy, He sent us His Son, that all may be grafted into the living Vine. (John 15:1-2)

What is a vine?   A vine is the stem which brings water to the branches, and it grows on the earth, and is hung on cross beams, and the vine can spread over large areas. And who is the Christ? He is the Vine (John 15:1), and the Truth and the Word. And He is the vine that brings water from the heavens. For He was a man, and tread on this earth, and was hung on the cross, that we may be saved. Christ the true Vine came to us all, and His Word has spread through the nations.

And who tends the grapevine? The grapevine must be tended by the vinedresser, for it is not able to hold itself up. And grapevines require watering and pruning, and they must be raised on supports to bear fruit. And the Vine of Christ must be pruned by the Vinedresser, for the Vinedresser of the Vine is the Father. (John 15:1-2). And He prunes the Vine, and gives it sustenance to grow. (Isaiah 27:2-3) And the Father gives support, that we may bear fruit.   And the grapevines are "layered" by lowering the vine, and forcing it to crawl on the earth, to grow roots and develop new grapevines. And the Father brings His children down to serve men, and puts them through trials that they may bear fruit.

And what is a branch? A branch is a stem that comes from the vine. And we are the branches, and the Vine is the Christ. For as the Lord said, "I am the vine, you are the branches." (John 15:5) And the vinedresser grafts in new branches, to give the grapevine variety and depth. And the Father has taken the vine of His people, and has grafted new branches from all of the nations. (Romans 11:19). But just as the Lord cut them off for their sins, so can He cut off the branches of the nations. (Romans 11:20). And just as the Lord grafts in all of the nations, so will He graft Israel back to the vine. (Romans 11:24)

But the time to bear fruits will come to an end. For those that bear fruits, the rewards will be great. But for those who bear none, will be burned in the fire. (John 15:5) And the fruit of the body shall be thrown in the winepress, and the wine of their blood shall fill all the land. (Revelation 14:18-20) And great is their fall, for they yielded no fruit, and refused to be branches of Christ the true Vine.

XII

We Produce the Grapes, the Fruit of Our Labor (NASB)
To Andrew the Prophet
Completed September 28, 2007

"The axe is already laid at the root of the trees; therefore every tree that does not bear good **fruit** is cut down and thrown into the fire." Matthew 3:10

God is the source of the fruit

"My **Father** is glorified by this, that you bear much **fruit**, and so prove to be My disciples." John 15:8

"And Jesus answered them, saying, 'The hour has come for the **Son** of Man to be glorified. Truly, truly, I say to you, unless a grain of wheat falls into the earth and dies, it remains alone; but if it dies, it bears much **fruit**.'" John 12:23-24

"But the **fruit** of the **Spirit** is love, joy, peace, patience, kindness, goodness, faithfulness, gentleness, self-control; against such things there is no law." Galatians 5:22-23

The first fruit of mankind was from the tree of knowledge

"Then God said, "Let the earth sprout vegetation, plants yielding seed, and **fruit** trees on the earth bearing **fruit** after their kind with seed in them"; and it was so." Genesis 1:11

"The woman said to the serpent, 'From the **fruit** of the trees of the garden we may eat; but from the **fruit** of the tree which is in the middle of the garden, God has said, 'You shall not eat from it or touch it, or you will die.'" Genesis 3:2

"Behold, children are a gift of the LORD, The **fruit** of the womb is a reward" Psalm 127:3

But the fruit of mankind failed

"No longer shall your name be called Abram, But your name shall be Abraham; For I have made you the father of a multitude of nations. I will make you exceedingly **fruitful**, and I will make nations of you, and kings will come forth from you." Genesis 17:5-7

"You shall bring the choice first **fruits** of your soil into the house of the LORD your God." Exodus 23:19

"Nor shall you glean your vineyard, nor shall you gather the fallen **fruit** of your vineyard; you shall leave them for the needy and for the stranger. I am the LORD your God." Leviticus 19:10

"If also after these things you do not obey Me, then I will punish you seven times more for your sins. 'I will also break down your pride of power; I will also make your sky like iron and your earth like bronze. Your strength will be spent uselessly, for your land will not yield its produce and the trees of the land will not yield their **fruit**." Leviticus 26:18-20

The Holy Spirit produces His fruit through us

"Truly, truly, I say to you, unless one is born of water and the Spirit he cannot enter into the kingdom of God. 'That which is born of the flesh is flesh, and that which is born of the Spirit is spirit.' Do not be amazed that I said to you, 'You must be born again .' The wind blows where it wishes and you hear the sound of it, but do not know where it comes from and where it is going; so is everyone who is born of the Spirit." John 3:5-8

"You will know them by their **fruits**. Grapes are not gathered from thorn bushes nor figs from thistles, are they? So every good tree bears good **fruit**, but the bad tree bears bad **fruit**. A good tree cannot produce bad **fruit**, nor can a bad tree produce good **fruit**."

"And the one on whom seed was sown on the good soil, this is the man who hears the word and understands it; who indeed bears **fruit** and brings forth, some a hundredfold, some sixty, and some thirty." Matthew 13:23

And the grapes are ready to be harvested

"He will drop off his unripe **grape** like the vine, And will cast off his flower like the olive tree. For the company of the godless is barren, And fire consumes the tents of the corrupt." Job 15:33

"Thus says the LORD of hosts, 'They will thoroughly glean as the vine the remnant of Israel; Pass your hand again like a **grape** gatherer Over the branches.'" Jeremiah 6:9

"What more was there to do for My vineyard that I have not done in it? Why, when I expected it to produce good **grapes** did it produce worthless ones? So now let Me tell you what I am going to do to My vineyard: I will remove its hedge and it will be consumed; I will break down its wall and it will become trampled ground." Isaiah 5:4-6

"Then I looked, and behold, the Lamb was standing on Mount Zion, and with Him one hundred and forty-four thousand, having His name and the name of His Father written on their foreheads...These have been purchased from among men as first **fruits** to God and to the Lamb. And no lie was found in their mouth; they are blameless." Revelation 14:1-5

"The axe is already laid at the root of the trees; therefore every tree that does not bear good **fruit** is cut down and thrown into the fire." Matthew 3:10

"For this is My blood of the covenant, which is poured out for many for forgiveness of sins. But I say to you, I will not drink of this **fruit** of the vine from now on until that day when I drink it new with you in My Father's kingdom." Matthew 26:28-29

"Then another angel, the one who has power over fire, came out from the altar; and he called with a loud voice to him who had the sharp sickle, saying, 'Put in your sharp sickle and gather the clusters from the vine of the earth, because her **grapes** are ripe.' So the angel swung his sickle to the earth and gathered the clusters from the vine of the earth, and threw them into the great wine press of the wrath of God. And the wine press was trodden outside the city, and blood came out from the wine press, up to the horses' bridles, for a distance of two hundred miles." Revelation 14:18-20

"Then he showed me a river of the water of life, clear as crystal, coming from the throne of God and of the Lamb, in the middle of its street. On either side of the river was the tree of life, bearing twelve kinds of **fruit**, yielding its **fruit** every month; and the leaves of the tree were for the healing of the nations." Revelation 22:1-2

The Fruits of the Labor

The Lord calls on us to produce His fruits, through the sustenance of the Father, the Word of the Son, and the gifts of the Holy Spirit. For the Father commands that we glorify His name, and are worthy disciples by producing His fruits. (John 15:8) For the Son of God descended as a man, and was crucified on the cross, that His fruits be manifest. (John 12:23-24) And the fruits of the Holy Spirit are of labor and sacrifice, "being love, joy, peace, patience, kindness, goodness, faithfulness, gentleness, and self-control." (Galatians 5:22-23)

The Father created the earth, and when He created the earth, He created the seed, the seed within the fruit, to spread through all the earth. (Genesis 1:11) And the fruit forbidden in the Garden of God, was the fruit of the knowledge of God, and Adam and Eve ate of that fruit. (Genesis 3:2) Yet despite their fall, they yielded great fruit, for through the fruit of knowledge, the seed of mankind was planted. And from that fruit, the seed of mankind spread to the nations, for the fruit of mankind was the fruit of the womb. (Psalm 127:3)

The fruit of the seed was promised through Abraham, for He was the father of the nations, the father of Islam, Judaism, and Christianity of their land, and to care for the needy. (Leviticus 19:10) But His people transgressed His commands, for they withheld the fruit of their sacrifice. And as the Lord had forewarned, "your land will not yield its produce and the trees of the land will not yield their fruit."(Leviticus 26:18-20)

And what is a fruit? A fruit is a ripened ovary, which when pollinated will grow. The fruits of the Holy Spirit are the works of the Holy Spirit. For when a follower of Christ is filled with the Holy Spirit, he is born of the Holy Spirit, and the fruits of the Spirit are manifest. (John 3:5-8) For the "good tree bears good fruit, but the bad tree bears bad fruit. A good tree cannot produce bad fruit, nor can a bad tree produce good fruit." (Matthew 7:16-18) And the fruits are as faceted as the nations, for the fruits of the earth are varied and colored. And the fruits of the Spirit are as faceted as the nations, for the Father has grafted all the nations into the Vine.

And how does a fruit spread its seed? The dispersal of a seed is as varied as the seeds. Some are consumed by animals, some are dispersed by the wind, while others can travel great distances by water. And the Seed of the Word is spread in manifold ways. As animals consume the seed of the fruit, the martyrs are consumed by their persecutors, that the Word of God may spread. As the wind disperses the seed, the Spirit disperses His followers, to produce His works and His fruit. And as water disperses the seed, the Father sustains His children, that they may yield His fruit. And the yield of the fruit is great. (Matthew 13:23)

But the time is nigh and the end is near. And did He not promise, in the days of our forefathers, that the day of the harvest would come? (Job 15:33) And did He not promise, in the days of the prophets, that He would gather His remnant, for they are the grapes that are blameless. (Jeremiah 6:9/ Revelation 14:1-5) And the grapes that are worthless shall also be harvested, but they shall be thrown out and crushed in the vineyard. (Isaiah 5:4-6) For "the axe is already laid at the root of the trees; therefore every tree that does not bear good fruit is cut down and thrown into the fire." (Matthew 3:10)

And what is the fruit of the vine? Christ has sacrificed the fruit of the vine, for He has sacrificed the wine of the Vine, for He has sacrificed the blood of His body. And recall His words at the table of sacrifice, "I will not drink of this fruit of the vine from now on until that day when I drink it new with you in My Father's kingdom." (Matthew 26:28-29) For when He returns, He will drink from the cup, the fruit of the vine. But this cup of the wine is anew, for this Cup will not hold the wine of His blood... **for this cup will hold the blood of mankind!** "And another angel came out of the temple which is in heaven, and he also had a sharp sickle. Then another angel, the one who has power over fire, came out from the altar; and he called with a loud voice to him who had the sharp sickle, saying, 'Put in your sharp sickle and gather the clusters from the vine of the earth, because her grapes are ripe.' So the angel swung his sickle to the earth and gathered the clusters from the vine of the earth, and threw them into the great wine press of the wrath of God. And the wine press was trodden outside the city, and blood came out from the wine press, up to the horses' bridles, for a distance of two hundred miles." (Revelation 14:17-20)

But the Father is loving and forgiving, and when all debts are paid in full, all will be reconciled back to His Vine. For His kingdom will be a resting place, and a healing place for all of the nations, and His fruit will give healing to the people. (Revelation 22:1-2) And to His glory and the fruit of His kingdom, we anxiously await.

XIII

God's Covenants: the Flood, the Cross, and the Fire (NASB)
To Andrew the Prophet
Completed October 2, 2007

The first covenant to mankind was with Water, the Father, a rainbow

"It shall come about, when I bring a cloud over the earth, that the bow will be seen in the cloud, and I will remember My **covenant**, which is between Me and you and every living creature of all flesh; and never again shall the water become a flood to destroy all flesh. When the bow is in the cloud, then I will look upon it, to remember the everlasting covenant between God and every living creature of all flesh that is on the earth. And God said to Noah, 'This is the sign of the **covenant** which I have established between Me and all flesh that is on the earth.'" Genesis 9:14-17

God makes a covenant with Israel

"Moses went up to God, and the LORD called to him from the mountain, saying, "Thus you shall say to the house of Jacob and tell the sons of Israel: You yourselves have seen what I did to the Egyptians, and how I bore you on eagles' wings, and brought you to Myself. Now then, if you will indeed obey My voice and keep My **covenant**, then you shall be My own possession among all the peoples, for all the earth is Mine; and you shall be to Me a kingdom of priests and a holy nation.' These are the words that you shall speak to the sons of Israel." Exodus 19:3-6

"So he was there with the LORD forty days and forty nights; he did not eat bread or drink water. And he wrote on the tablets the words of the **covenant**, the Ten Commandments." Exodus 34:28

But Israel failed His covenant

"You shall make no **covenant** with them or with their gods. They shall not live in your land, because they will make you sin against Me; for if you serve their gods, it will surely be a snare to you." Exodus 23:32-33

"Do we not all have one father? Has not one God created us? Why do we deal treacherously each against his brother so as to profane the **covenant** of our fathers?" Malachi 2:10

"Yet you say, 'For what reason?' Because the LORD has been a witness between you and the wife of your youth, against whom you have dealt treacherously, though she is your companion and your wife by **covenant**." Malachi 2:14-16

"Behold, I am going to send My messenger, and he will clear the way before Me. And the Lord, whom you seek, will suddenly come to His temple; and the messenger of the **covenant**, in whom you delight, behold, He is coming," says the LORD of hosts." Malachi 3:1-4

"Yes, Father, for this way was well-pleasing in Your sight. 'All things have been handed over to Me by My Father, and no one knows who the **Son** is except the Father, and who the Father is except the **Son**, and anyone to whom the **Son** wills to reveal Him.'" Luke 10:21-22

The second covenant with mankind was with Blood, the Son, the Cross

"And when He had taken a cup and given thanks, He gave it to them, saying, 'Drink from it, all of you; for this is My blood of the **covenant**, which is poured out for many for forgiveness of sins.'" Matthew 26:27

"They took Jesus, therefore, and He went out, bearing His own **cross**, to the place called the Place of a Skull, which is called in Hebrew, Golgotha." John 19:17

"It was the third hour when they **crucified** Him. The inscription of the charge against Him read, 'THE KING OF THE JEWS.' And Jesus uttered a loud cry, and breathed His last. And the veil of the temple was torn in two from top to bottom." Mark 15:25-37

"Men of Israel, listen to these words: Jesus the Nazarene, a man attested to you by God with miracles and wonders and signs which God performed through Him in your midst, just as you yourselves know-- this Man, delivered over by the predetermined plan and foreknowledge of God, you nailed to a **cross** by the hands of godless men and put Him to death. But God raised Him up again, putting an end to the agony of death, since it was impossible for Him to be held in its power." Acts 2:22-24

"I will ask the Father, and He will give you another Helper, that He may be with you forever; that is the **Spirit** of truth, whom the world cannot receive, because it does not see Him or know Him, but you know Him because He abides with you and will be in you." John 14:16-17

"And he who does not take his **cross** and follow after Me is not worthy of Me. He who has found his life will lose it, and he who has lost his life for My sake will find it." Matthew 10:38

"For this reason He is the mediator of a new **covenant**, so that, since a death has taken place for the redemption of the transgressions that were committed under the first **covenant**, those who have been called may receive the promise of the eternal inheritance. For where a **covenant** is, there must of necessity be the death of the one who made it. For a **covenant** is valid only when men are dead, for it is never in force while the one who made it lives." Hebrew 9:15-17

And the third and final covenant with mankind will be the Fire, the Spirit, GOD

"And the nations were enraged, and Your wrath came, and the time came for the dead to be judged, and the time to reward Your bond-servants the prophets and the saints and those who fear Your name, the small and the great, and to destroy those who destroy the earth. And the temple of God which is in heaven was opened; and the ark of His **covenant** appeared in His temple, and there were flashes of lightning and sounds and peals of thunder and an earthquake and a great hailstorm." Revelation 11:18-19

"And I heard a voice from heaven, saying, 'Write, 'Blessed are the dead who die in the Lord from now on!' 'Yes,' says the **Spirit**, 'so that they may rest from their labors, for their deeds follow with them.'" Revelation 14:13

"The **Spirit** and the bride say, 'Come.' And let the one who hears say, 'Come.' And let the one who is thirsty come; let the one who wishes take the water of life without cost." Revelation 22:17

There will be three covenants: the Flood, the Cross, and the Fire

What are the covenants? A covenant is a promise made from God to mankind, paid with a sacrifice, and sealed with a sign. The first covenant with mankind was through Noah, and the sacrifice was mankind's death through the flood, and the sign was a rainbow from the sun in the clouds. (Genesis 9:14-17) Because of the sins of mankind, a sacrifice was made with the water, the power that is held by the Father. His sign of the covenant was a rainbow, which is created by the water and the sun. And through this covenant He promised, not to destroy man by water again, until the light of the rainbow was gone. And ironically the source of the rainbow is the sun, for during the wrath the sun will not give its light. "Then the fifth angel poured out his bowl on the throne of the beast, and his kingdom became darkened." (Revelation 16:10)

And the Lord made a covenant with Israel. (Exodus 19:3-6). For He promised they would be a great nation, and the sacrifice was the blood of the Egyptians, and the sign was the Ten Commandments. (Exodus 34:28) And this covenant was made on the promise, that they would obey His commandments. But they transgressed His

commandments, for they worshiped false idols. (Exodus 23:32-33) punished the faithless, and cut off their branch from His Vine. And God promised to send us His Son, to make a new covenant with mankind. (Malachi 3:1-4) For when His Son came, all things would be handed from the Father to the Son. (Luke 10:21-22)

And the second covenant with _mankind_ was made through the Son, and the sacrifice was His blood, and His sign was a cross. For Christ the Son has brought the Word, and by His death and crucifixion, the Holy Spirit could dwell with us. And the new covenant is this, that the gates of heaven would be opened, and that all men could enter His kingdom.(Matthew 26:27) And His sacrifice was offered at the table, for He said "'This is My body which is given for you; do this in remembrance of Me.' And in the same way He took the cup after they had eaten, saying, 'This cup which is poured out for you is the new covenant in My blood.'" (Luke 22:19-20) And as Christ carried His cross, so must we bear our cross. (John 19:17) And our Lord was nailed to the cross, and covered the sins of mankind. (Mark 15:25-37) And when He died the Spirit left Him. And as He "breathed His last", the Light left the world, and the Father's veil was torn in two. "It was now about the sixth hour, and darkness fell over the whole land until the ninth hour, because the sun was obscured; and the veil of the temple was torn in two." (Luke 23:44-45) And after His death, the water from His Father, would depart from His body. "But one of the soldiers pierced His side with a spear, and immediately blood and water came out." (John 19:34) But the Father raised His Son to the heavens, and He opened the gates of the heavens, that those who would follow may enter. And the Son sent the Spirit to dwell amongst us. (Acts 2:22-24) And all things would be handed from the Son to the Spirit.

For Christ has sacrificed His life, that we could find life with the Father. And He paid the price by denying Himself, and we as His children must do the same. For those who do follow Him, must take up their cross, of sacrifice and death to this world. For "he who has found his life will lose it, and he who has lost his life for My sake will find it." (Matthew 10:38) But few have the faith and the courage of Christ, for the price of the cross is persecution and death.

"For a covenant is valid only when men are dead, for it is never in force while the one who made it lives." (Hebrew 9:15-17)

And what is a cross? A cross is an intersection between God and man, for where God and man meet a covenant is made. And a cross is an upright post, with a transverse cross near the top, on which persecuted prisoners are executed. And Christ the Son of God, was crucified on the cross. And the symbol of the cross is the Greek letter tau (τ). And tau is a fascinating mathematical number.

In the theory of relativity tau is the symbol for *proper time*. Proper time (τ) is distinguished from coordinate time (t). Coordinate time is time as we know it, as it exists in this earthly realm. Proper time is measured by a single clock between events that occur at the same place as the clock. It depends not only on the events but also on the motion of the clock between the events. If the clock remains at rest, the time that is measured is coordinate time. However, if the clock moves at a higher velocity, then the time between the two events is shortened, and this is measured as proper time. And this has been scientifically proven, for due to its velocity, the clock on the International Space Station runs slower than the earth's clock. And so does "time in heaven" exist in a different time frame than "time on earth." For the realm that we live is in coordinate time, and those committed to this earth have remained on "time on earth". And as we know, Christ is the Light. So after their deaths in this realm, His followers have entered the realm of the heavens, and thus they travel at the speed of "Light" and have entered a "time in heaven." And those who have not followed Christ, after their death have been committed to "time on earth". And those that have persecuted Christ and His followers, after their death have been committed to "time in hell". And now that the end is near, all have been brought back to the earth, so that all may receive their just due.

In mathematics, tau is the symbol for the *golden ratio*. This number is the ratio that artists and architects have strived for, because this proportion is considered both aesthetically and divinely pleasing. for this number are *the divine proportion, the divine* if the ratio between the sum of those quantities and the larger one is the same as the ratio between the larger one and the smaller. The golden ratio is approximately 1.6180339887. In other words:

$$\frac{a}{a=larger\ quantity} \qquad \frac{b}{b=smaller\ quantity}$$

$$a + b\,/\,a\ = a/b\ =\ \tau\ =\ 1.\,6\,1\,8.\,.\,.\,.$$

And if we look at the most beautiful architecture in the world, the divine ratio has been put to use: The Great Pyramids of Egypt, Parthenon in Athens, Porch of Maidens in Athens, Chartres Cathedral, Cathedral of Notre Dame, Le Corbussier. And if we look at the most beautiful paintings of the world, the divine ratio has been used: *An Old Man* - Da Vinci, *The Vetruvian Man* - Da Vinci, *Mona Lisa* - Da Vinci, *Holy Family* - Michelangelo, *Last Supper* - DaVinci, *Crucifixion* - Raphael, *Self Portrait* - Rembrandt, *Sacrament of the Last Supper* - Dali, *Bathers* - Seurat, the Mondrian compositions, and the list goes on. And if we look at the most beautiful structures in nature, the divine ratio has been used: the spiral of the nautilus, the tusks of rams and elephants, the growth curvature of flowers, the spiral of pine cones, and of course, the human body (the human form, the human face, and the structure of DNA).

The Golden Ratio

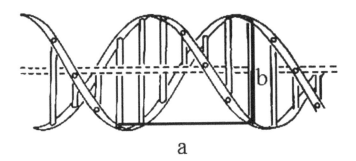

Structure of DNA

Pyramids of Egypt

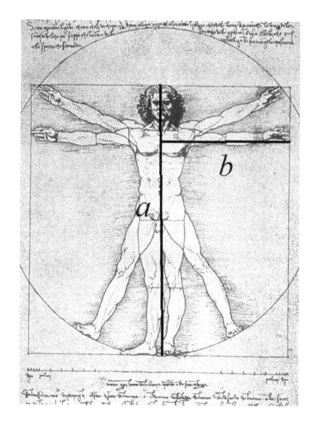

The Vetruvian Man

The question is does this ratio apply to God's covenants? If we substitute a for the time from the covenant of Noah to the birth of Christ, and b for the time from the birth of Christ to the fire of judgment we get:

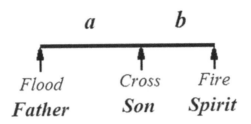

Hence we can calculate the dates as follows:

The date of the flood: "And we found the account of creation, and at what time he made the heaven and the earth and the first man Adam, and that from thence to flood, were **two thousand, two hundred and twelve years**. And from the f lood to Abraham, nine hundred and twelve. And from Abraham to Moses, four hundred and thirty. And from Moses to David the king, five hundred and ten. And from David to the Babylonish captivity, five hundred years. And from the Babylonish captivity to the incarnation of Christ, four hundred years. The sum of which amounts to **five thousand and half."** (Nicodemus 22:16-19)

Thus, the date of the flood = the date of Adam (5500 years before His crucifixion) - the date from Adam to the flood (2212 years) - age of Christ at His crucifixion (30 years) = **3258 BC**

The date of Christ's birth: **0 AD**

The date of the fire of judgment: *to be determined*

If   a = 3258 BC

Then b = time from the Christ's birth to the end of the world

= 2013.59 AD

Interestingly, this date is August 2013, the end of the 7 year period after the arrival of the anti-Christ, Moqtada al-Sadr.   This date also coincides with the end of the world on the Mayan and Aztec Calenders.

Thus the end time is near, and the final covenant shall be made. And the sacrifice will be the blood of mankind. (Revelation 11:18-19) And each man will get His just recompense, and after each cent has been paid, then all will be able to enter His kingdom. (Revelation 14:13) And the sign is a sign that will remain with us forever, for the sign is the presence of God in our midst. And the Spirit will hand all things back to the Father, and the circle will then be complete.   And "there will no longer be any curse; and the throne of God and of the Lamb will be in it, and His bond-servants will serve Him; they will see His face, and His name will be on their foreheads". (Revelation 22:3-4) And the Holy Spirit and martyrs, and the prophets and saints, and the Son and the Father, will say "Come". (Revelation 22:17)

HOLY SPIRIT

2013
AD

S Ø N

3258
BC

FATHER

Covenants of the Cross

XIV

The True Wine is the Holy Spirit (NKJV)
To Andrew the Prophet
October 4, 2010

Wine brings gladness to the heart, and heartbreak

"You cause the grass to grow for the cattle, and plants for people to use, to bring forth food from the earth, and **wine** to gladden the human heart" Psalms 104:14-15

"**Wine** is a mocker, strong drink a brawler, and whoever is led astray by it is not wise." Proverbs 20:1

Wine has mediated the curses of mankind

"He drank some of the **wine** and became drunk, and he lay uncovered in his tent. And Ham, the father of Canaan, saw the nakedness of his father, and told his two brothers outside. Then Shem and Japheth took a garment, laid it on both their shoulders, and walked backward and covered the nakedness of their father; their faces were turned away, and they did not see their father's nakedness. When Noah awoke from his **wine** and knew what his youngest son had done to him, he said, 'Cursed be Canaan; lowest of slaves shall he be to his brothers.'" Genesis 9:21-25

"So they made their father drink **wine** that night also; and the younger rose, and lay with him; and he did not know when she lay down or when she rose. Thus both the daughters of Lot became pregnant by their father. The firstborn bore a son, and named him Moab; he is the ancestor of the Moabites to this day. The younger also bore a son and named him Ben-ammi; he is the ancestor of the Ammonites to this day." Genesis 19:35-38

"He said, 'Are you really my son Esau?' He answered, 'I am.' Then he said, 'Bring it to me, that I may eat of my son's game and bless you.' So he brought it to him, and he ate; and he brought him **wine**, and he drank. Then his father Isaac said to him, 'Come near and kiss me, my son.'" Genesis 17:24-25

"Whoever loves pleasure will suffer want; whoever loves **wine** and oil will not be rich." Proverbs 21:17

The priests and prophets were instructed to stay away from wine

"Do not be among **winebibbers**, or among gluttonous eaters of meat; for the drunkard and the glutton will come to poverty, and drowsiness will clothe them with rags." Proverbs 23:20-21

"And the Lord spoke to Aaron: Drink no **wine** or strong drink, neither you nor your sons, when you enter the tent of meeting, that you may not die; it is a statute forever throughout your generations." Leviticus 10:8-9

"But the angel said to him, 'Do not be afraid, Zechariah, for your prayer has been heard. Your wife Elizabeth will bear you a son, and you will name him John. You will have joy and gladness, and many will rejoice at his birth, for he will be great in the sight of the Lord. He must never drink **wine** or strong drink; even before his birth he will be filled with the Holy Spirit." Luke 1:13-15

Mankind failed and the Lord promised to trample the vineyard

"What more was there to do for my vineyard that I have not done in it? When I expected it to yield grapes, why did it yield wild grapes? And now I will tell you what I will do to my vineyard. I will remove its hedge, and it shall be devoured; I will break down its wall, and it shall be trampled down." Isaiah 5:4-5

"Thus says the Lord: As the **wine** is found in the cluster, and they say, 'Do not destroy it, for there is a blessing in it,' so I will do for

"There is an outcry in the streets for lack of **wine**; all joy has reached its eventide; the gladness of the earth is banished. Desolation is left in the city, the gates are battered into ruins. For thus it shall be on the earth and among the nations, as when an olive tree is beaten, as at the gleaning when the grape harvest is ended." Isaiah 24:11-13

"I will make your oppressors eat their own flesh, and they shall be drunk with their own blood as with **wine**. Then all flesh shall know that I am the Lord your Savior, and your Redeemer, the Mighty One of Jacob" Isaiah 49:26

Christ came to give us His Wine

"Jesus said to them, 'Fill the jars with water.' And they filled them up to the brim. He said to them, 'Now draw some out, and take it to the chief steward.; So they took it. When the steward tasted the water that had become **wine**, and did not know where it came from (though the servants who had drawn the water knew), the steward called the bridegroom and said to him, 'Everyone serves the good **wine** first, and then the inferior wine after the guests have become drunk. But you have kept the good **wine** until now.'" John 2:7-1

"He also told them a parable: 'No one tears a piece from a new garment and sews it on an old garment; otherwise the new will be torn, and the piece from the new will not match the old. And no one puts new **wine** into old **wineskins**; otherwise the new **wine** will burst the skins and will be spilled, and the skins will be destroyed. But new **wine** must be put into fresh **wineskins**. And no one after drinking old **wine** desires new **wine**, but says, 'The old is good.'" Luke 5:36-39

"Then he took a cup, and after giving thanks he said, 'Take this and divide it among yourselves; for I tell you that from now on I will not drink of the fruit of the vine until the kingdom of God comes.'" Luke 22:17-18

The Holy Spirit is the new Wine

"Do not get drunk with **wine**, for that is debauchery; but be filled with the Spirit, as you sing psalms and hymns and spiritual songs among yourselves, singing and making melody to the Lord in your hearts, giving thanks to God the Father at all times and for everything in the name of our Lord Jesus Christ." Ephesians 5:18-20

Then He will harvest the earth, and great is the wrath

"Put in the sickle, for the harvest is ripe. Go in, tread, for the **wine** press is full. The vats overflow, for their wickedness is great." Joel 3:13

"So the angel swung his sickle over the earth and gathered the vintage of the earth, and he threw it into the great **wine** press of the wrath of God. And the wine press was trodden outside the city, and blood flowed from the **wine** press, as high as a horse's bridle, for a distance of about two hundred miles." Revelation 14:19-20

But all men will be reconciled

"Ho, everyone who thirsts, come to the waters; and you that have no money, come, buy and eat! Come, buy **wine** and milk without money and without price." Isaiah 55:1

"So you shall know that I, the Lord your God, dwell in Zion, my holy mountain. And Jerusalem shall be holy, and strangers shall never again pass through it. In that day the mountains shall drip sweet **wine**, the hills shall flow with milk, and all the stream beds of Judah shall flow with water; a fountain shall come forth from the house of the Lord and water the Wadi Shittim." Joel 3:17-18

Wine is a mocker, True Wine is blood

Wine is a spirit, which in moderation brings gladness, but in excess causes heartbreak. For wine can "gladden the human heart"; (Psalm 104:14-15) but wine in excess "is a mocker", and "whoever is led astray by it is not wise." (Proverbs 20:1) For the fall of man is traced back to wine, a spirit which has led men astray. And one does not have to look far, to see what great harm wine has done. For the Palestinians to this day, live with the curse of Canaan, for day, live with the curse of Lot, for in a drunken state he slept with his daughters. (Genesis 19:35-38) And the countries of Islam to this day, suffer from the curse of Esau, whose inheritance was stolen by Jacob, while his father lay drunk. (Genesis 17:24-25)   And even to this day, the curse of wine continues on, for as the end comes near, the curse has transferred to the Bush administration , but "whoever loves pleasure will suffer want; whoever loves *wine and oil* will not be rich." (Proverbs 21:17)

Due to the evils of wine, the priests and prophets were instructed, not to drink wine because of its spirit. For the prophets already knew, they had inherited all of God's riches, but through the mockery of wine could lose their inheritance with God. (Proverbs 23:20-21) And Aaron the first of the priests, and the following generations, were instructed by God not to drink from the wine, when they entered His tent of worship. (Leviticus 10:8-9).   And the prophet John the Baptist, was instructed not to fill, his body with any wine, but be filled with the Spirit. (Luke 1:13-15)

But the Lord's people failed Him, and for their vast indulgence, He removed their land and trampled their vineyard. (Isaiah 5:4-5) And He promised that the day would come, when He would harvest His people, the grapes of His blessing. (Isaiah 65:8-9) But when they are risen, the grape harvest will end, and destruction will devour mankind. (Isaiah 24:11-13) And His judgment is just, for the wrath is not caused by God's hand, but the wrath comes from the hand of mankind; for mankind will eat their own flesh, and they will drink their own blood. (Isaiah 49:26)

And God in His mercy, sent His only Son to bring us the Wine, and to give His blood as a sacrifice for mankind. And at the wedding, the Groom changed water into wine, for as the steward said, the Father has "kept the good Wine until now." (John 2:7-1) For the good Wine came to earth, to place new wine into new wineskins; for He came to graft all the nations into the Vine. And though all the nations have been grafted in the Vine, His first love remains for His people. For His first love is for Judah and His second love is for Israel, for like the old wine that is stored in old wineskins, "the old is good". (Luke 5:36-39) And before He died, He promised not to drink the wine until He came again, for the new wine is the blood of mankind. (Luke 22:17-18)

Christ was crucified on the cross, that we may receive the Holy Spirit. And He commands us not to be filled with the spirit of wine, but to be filled with the Spirit of God. And no longer are we filled with songs of debauchery, but with songs of thanksgiving and praise.(Ephesians 5:18-20)

But now the end has come. When Christ the King returns, He will harvest His prophets and martyrs and saints, the temple of God and the tribe of Judah, the creature with four heads and the unblemished grapes. For His temple is perfect and "no fault could be found in them". (Revelation 14:5). But that day is foreboding, for those left behind. But who can question His judgment, for had He not warned of this day, through the prophets that the judgment would come? (Joel 3:13) For Christ will harvest the unfinished grapes, and He will crush them in the winepress, and the blood of mankind will flow like the wine. (Revelation 14:19-20) And woe to those who are left behind!

And how is wine made from grapes? First it is crushed in the winepress, then it is fermented into wine, and then it is stored until it has matured. And what is the process of fermentation? Fermentation is the process through which sugar is consumed, under anaerobic conditions (without oxygen) and made into wine, and the CO2 and energy are disposed of. And the wrath of God is a process, through which mankind is consumed, in the absence of the Holy Spirit (oxygen), and made into the blood of mankind (wine), while the spirit (CO2) and body of man (energy) is thrown out. In other words:

$$C_6H_{12}O_6 \Rightarrow 2CH_3CH_2OH + 2CO2 + 2 \text{ ATP}$$

or

or

Mankind $\Rightarrow$ Blood of man + Spirit of man + Body of man

And the storage of wine is so wine can mature, by removing its excess debris. And the wrath will continue until each penny is paid, for as the Lord promised, "Truly I tell you, you will never get out until you have paid the last penny." (Matthew 5:26). And the times will be devastating indeed, for many will try to seek death, but as the prophecy says, "people will seek death but will not find it; they will long to die, but death will flee from them." (Revelation 5:6)

But when the last penny is paid, and the King drinks of the new wine, the gates will be opened for all, to drink of the wine of the Spirit. (Isaiah 55:1) All of the nations will live in peace, and the mountains will drip with sweet wine. And the Lord will dwell amongst us forever. (Joel 3:17-18)

X V

We will be the Rainbow (NKJV)
To Andrew the Prophet
Completed October 6, 2007

The Rainbow, The Promise

"I set My **rainbow** in the cloud, and it shall be for the sign of the covenant between Me and the earth. It shall be, when I bring a cloud over the earth, that the rainbow shall be seen in the cloud; and I will remember My covenant which is between Me and you and every living creature of all flesh; the waters shall never again become a flood to destroy all flesh. The **rainbow** shall be in the cloud, and I will look on it to remember the everlasting covenant between God and every living creature of all flesh that is on the earth. And God said to Noah, 'This is the sign of the covenant which I have established between Me and all flesh that is on the earth.'" Genesis 9:13-17

"Like the appearance of a **rainbow** in a cloud on a rainy day, so was the appearance of the brightness all around it. This was the appearance of the likeness of the glory of the Lord. So when I saw it, I fell on my face, and I heard a voice of One speaking." Ezekiel 1:28

"Immediately I was in the Spirit; and behold, a throne set in heaven, and One sat on the throne. And He who sat there was like a jasper and a sardius stone in appearance; and there was a **rainbow** around the throne, in appearance like an emerald." Revelation 4:2-3

Light is the source of the rainbow, Christ the Light is the source of life

Rain perfects His children

"For after seven more days I will cause it to **rain** on the earth forty days and forty nights, and I will destroy from the face of the earth all living things that I have made." Genesis 7:3

"But I say to you, love your enemies, bless those who curse you, do good to those who hate you, and pray for those who spitefully use you and persecute you, that you may be sons of your Father in heaven; for He makes His sun rise on the evil and on the good, and sends **rain** on the just and on the unjust. For if you love those who love you, what reward have you? Do not even the tax collectors do the same? And if you greet your brethren only, what do you do more than others? Do not even the tax collectors do so? Therefore you shall be perfect, just as your Father in heaven is perfect." Matthew 5:44-48

The Light produces His kingdom of many colors

"Now for the house of my God I have prepared with all my might: gold for things to be made of gold, silver for things of silver, bronze for things of bronze, iron for things of iron, wood for things of wood, onyx stones, stones to be set, glistening stones of various **colors**, all kinds of precious stones, and marble slabs in abundance." 1 Chronicles 29:2

"The royal daughter is all glorious within the palace; Her clothing is woven with gold. She shall be brought to the King in robes of many **colors**; The virgins, her companions who follow her, shall be brought to You. With gladness and rejoicing they shall be brought; They shall enter the King's palace." Psalms 45:13

"Now as I looked at the living creatures, behold, a wheel was on the earth beside each living creature with its four faces. The appearance of the wheels and their works was like the **color** of beryl, and all four had the same likeness. The appearance of their works was, as it were, a wheel in the middle of a wheel..The likeness of the firmament above the heads of the living creatures was like the color of an awesome crystal, stretched out over their heads." Ezekiel 1:15-22

"Then he measured its wall: one hundred and forty-four cubits, according to the measure of a man, that is, of an angel. And the construction of its wall was of jasper; and the city was pure gold, like clear glass. And the foundations of the wall of the city were adorned with all kinds of precious stones: the first foundation was jasper, the second sapphire, the third chalcedony, the fourth emerald, the fifth sardonyx, the sixth sardius, the seventh chrysolite, the eighth beryl, the ninth topaz, the tenth chrysoprase, the eleventh jacinth, and the twelfth amethyst. And the twelve gates were twelve pearls: each individual gate was of one pearl. And the street of the city was pure gold, like transparent glass. But I saw no temple in it, for the Lord God Almighty and the Lamb are its temple. And the city had no need of the sun or of the moon to shine in it, for the glory of God illuminated it, and the Lamb is its light. And the nations of those who are saved shall walk in its light, and the kings of the earth bring their glory and honor into it." Revelation 21:17-24

The rainbow, the spectrum of twelve, of the new kingdom

jasper-green sapphire-indigo chalcedony-yellow emerald-green sardonyx-orange sardius chrysolite-green beryl-gray topaz-yellow chrysoprase-red jacinth-orange amethyst-violet

The Rainbow: A Covenant for All

When the flood came down mankind was destroyed, but God saved mankind through Noah. And the Lord in His kindness, made a promise to man, that water would not kill them again. (Genesis 9:13-17) When the Lord appeared to Ezekiel, He was surrounded by a rainbow, a promise that the Lamb would come, and the temple of His body would be rebuilt. (Ezekiel 1:28) And when the Lord appeared to John, to foretell of the judgment to come, He was surrounded by a rainbow, a promise that the Lion would return, and the temple of His saints would be rebuilt. (Revelation 4:2-3)

And what is a rainbow? A rainbow is an arc with a spectrum of colors (identified as red, orange, yellow, green, blue, indigo, and

And before the covenant with Noah, God said to Noah, "The end of all flesh has come before Me, for the earth is filled with violence through them; and behold, I will destroy them with the earth. Make yourself an **ark** of gopherwood; make rooms in the **ark**, and cover it inside and outside with pitch." (Genesis 6:13-14). And the Lord instructed Noah, to save mankind by building an ark. And after the flood and mankind was saved, the arc of the rainbow was left as a covenant of God's mercy and grace.

The source of the rainbow is light from the sun. And in His mercy and kindness, God sent His Son into this world, to give Light to save mankind. And the source of God's covenant, is Light from the Son, for as He would say, "I am the light of the world. He who follows Me shall not walk in darkness, but have the light of life." (John 8:12)

How is sunlight refracted in a rainbow? The sunlight passes through a prism, which is created by rain. And before God created the first rainbow, it rained for forty days and nights. (Genesis 7:3) And the Son of God calls on His children, to be light of the world, for as He said, "You are the light of the world." (Matthew 5:14) And He causes His children to pass through the rain, for the rain is the persecution and trials, that His children must endure on this earth. And God commands us to go through the rain, that we may be perfected in His image, for when we endure these trials, we also will become perfect. (Matthew 5:44-48)

What is the spectrum of the rainbow? A spectrum is the distribution of visible light, into its component wavelengths and energy. And visible light is white, and the sum of its parts is its spectrum, which is broken down into seven colors: red, orange, yellow, green, blue, indigo, violet. And what was white becomes colorful like a rainbow. And the first temple of God was a prelude, of the beauty that His true temple would be (the 144,000), for it was adorned with precious stones of all colors. (1 Chronicles 29:2) And the psalmist promised that the royal daughter (the 144,000), would be adorned in robes of all colors. (Psalms 45:13) And the prophet foretold the creature with four heads (the 144,000) would have works of all colors, for their sacrifice for the Lord was great indeed. (Ezekiel 1:15-22)

And the glories of His temple is the rainbow of His kingdom. For like the temple of 144,000, it will measure 144 angelic cubits. (Revelation 21:17) And like the twelve tribes of Israel (12 X 12,000), the new kingdom will have twelve gates of pearls, which will be guarded by His twelve apostles. (Revelation 21:22) And like the color of their robes and their works, the walls of the city will be adorned, with jewels of many magnificent colors.(Revelation 21:18-21) And like the Light that has guided the temple, the city will be glorified by the Light. And all men and women, from all of the nations, will glorify and honor His majesty forever. (Revelation 21:22-24)

XVI

Seven Trumpets: A Harmonious Warning of the Judgment (NASB)
To Andrew the Prophet
Completed October 10, 2007

Music is a special prayer through the Holy Spirit

"It happened as they were coming, when David returned from killing the Philistine, that the women came out of all the cities of Israel, singing and dancing, to meet King Saul, with tambourines, with joy and with **musical** instruments." 1 Samuel 18:6

"It is good to give thanks to the LORD And to sing praises to Your name, O Most High; To declare Your lovingkindness in the morning And Your faithfulness by night, With the ten-stringed lute and with the harp, With resounding **music** upon the lyre. For You, O LORD, have made me glad by what You have done, I will sing for joy at the works of Your hands. How great are Your works, O LORD! Your thoughts are very deep." Psalms 92:1-5

Melody praises the Lord

"Shout joyfully to the LORD, all the earth; Break forth and sing for joy and sing praises. Sing praises to the LORD with the lyre, With the lyre and the sound of **melody**." Psalms 98:4-5

"Be filled with the Spirit, speaking to one another in psalms and hymns and spiritual songs, singing and making **melody** with your heart to the Lord" Ephesians 5:18-19

"Indeed, the LORD will comfort Zion; He will comfort all her waste places. And her wilderness He will make like Eden, And her desert like the garden of the LORD; Joy and gladness will be found in her, Thanksgiving and sound of a **melody**." Isaiah 51:3

Harmony shows the unity of music and spirit

"To sum up, all of you be **harmonious**, sympathetic, brotherly, kindhearted, and humble in spirit; not returning evil for evil or insult for insult, but giving a blessing instead; for you were called for the very purpose that you might inherit a blessing." 1 Peter 3:8-9

"Do not be bound together with unbelievers; for what partnership have righteousness and lawlessness, or what fellowship has light with darkness? Or what **harmony** has Christ with Belial, or what has a believer in common with an unbeliever?" 2 Corinthians 6:14-15

"If I speak with the tongues of men and of angels, but do not have love, I have become a noisy gong or a clanging **cymbal**." 1 Corinthians 13:1

The trumpet was used as a warning

"Now Mount Sinai was all in smoke because the LORD descended upon it in fire; and its smoke ascended like the smoke of a furnace, and the whole mountain quaked violently. When the sound of the **trumpet** grew louder and louder, Moses spoke and God answered him with thunder. The LORD came down on Mount Sinai, to the top of the mountain; and the LORD called Moses to the top of the mountain, and Moses went up." Exodus 19:18-20

"The LORD spoke further to Moses, saying,'Make yourself two **trumpets** of silver, of hammered work you shall make them; and you shall use them for summoning the congregation and for having the camps set out... When you go to war in your land against the adversary who attacks you, then you shall sound an alarm with the **trumpets**, that you may be remembered before the LORD your God, and be saved from your enemies.'" Numbers 10:1-8

"You shall march around the city, all the men of war circling the city once. You shall do so for six days. Also seven priests shall carry trumpets of rams' horns before the ark; then on the seventh times and the priests shall blow the **trumpets**. It shall be that when they make a long blast with the ram's horn, and when you hear the sound of the trumpet, all the people shall shout with a great shout; and the wall of the city will fall down flat, and the people will go up every man straight ahead." Joshua 6:3-7

And the final seven trumpets will sound

"With **trumpets** and the sound of the horn Shout joyfully before the King, the LORD. Let the sea roar and all it contains, The world and those who dwell in it. Let the rivers clap their hands, Let the mountains sing together for joy Before the LORD, for He is coming to judge the earth; He will judge the world with righteousness And the peoples with equity." Psalms 98: 6-9

"Blow a **trumpet** in Zion, And sound an alarm on My holy mountain! Let all the inhabitants of the land tremble, For the day of the LORD is coming; Surely it is near, A day of darkness and gloom, A day of clouds and thick darkness. As the dawn is spread over the mountains, So there is a great and mighty people; There has never been anything like it, Nor will there be again after it To the years of many generations." Joel 2:1-2

"And then the sign of the Son of Man will appear in the sky, and then all the tribes of the earth will mourn, and they will see the SON OF MAN COMING ON THE CLOUDS OF THE SKY with power and great glory. And He will send forth His angels with A GREAT **TRUMPET** and THEY WILL GATHER TOGETHER His elect from the four winds, from one end of the sky to the other." Matthew 24:30-31

"When the Lamb broke the seventh seal, there was silence in heaven for about half an hour. And I saw the seven angels who stand before God, and seven **trumpets** were given to them... And the seven angels who had the seven **trumpets** prepared themselves to sound them..Then the angel whom I saw standing on the sea and on the land lifted up his right hand to heaven, and swore by Him who lives forever and ever, WHO CREATED HEAVEN AND THE THINGS IN IT, AND THE EARTH AND THE THINGS IN IT, AND THE

SEA AND THE THINGS IN IT, that there will be delay no longer, but in the days of the voice of the seventh angel, when he is about to sound, then the mystery of God is finished, as He preached to His servants the prophets...Then the seventh angel sounded; and there were loud voices in heaven, saying, 'The kingdom of the world has become the kingdom of our Lord and of His Christ; and He will reign forever and ever.'" Revelation 8:1-11:15

"Behold, I tell you a mystery; we will not all sleep, but we will all be changed, in a moment, in the twinkling of an eye, at the last **trumpet**; for the **trumpet** will sound, and the dead will be raised imperishable, and we will be changed. For this perishable must put on the imperishable, and this mortal must put on immortality." 1 Corinthians 15:51-53

The Last Seal: The Trumpets Will Sound

Music transcends our words, for through the voice of the Spirit, the Father can hear our voice. Music is based on chordal harmonics, and the melody of the instrument's voice. It is also the language of the Holy Spirit, unaltered by the Tower of Babel; for music is the universal language, spoken and heard by all people. And His people used music to rejoice, when they were victorious in battle. (1 Samuel 18:6) And music is a means of rejoicing, for God's loving kindness and faithfulness. (Psalms 92:1-5) For through the music the Spirit intercedes, and transforms our broken language, into prayers that are worthy of the Father, "for we do not know how to pray as we should, but the Spirit Himself intercedes for us with groanings too deep for words." (Romans 8:26)

Music is divided into two different voices, a melodic and harmonic voice. Melody is the voice which raises our words, and praises the Lord with joy and thanksgiving, with the instruments and voices of the body. (Psalms 98:4-5) Melody transforms the words of the hymns, and fills our hearts with the Spirit. (Ephesians 5:18-19) For on that day His people will sing, with melodies of joy and

Harmony is the resonant tones that occur with any note , which is produced by any voice or instrument. Harmony is a series of musical tones, whose frequencies are multiples of the fundamental tone. And through the frequency of harmonics, subsequent notes are integrated in unison, which makes tonal music pleasing to the ear. Harmonics follows the physics of series progression as follows:

$$Harmonic\ note = \frac{1}{n!} = \text{where n represent the number of harmonic frequencies}$$

And in fact, our cochlear apparatus is physiologically structured, to respond to sound waves logarithmically. And the first harmonic or fundamental tone, has one sinusoidal wave form. The second harmonic or octave tone, has two wave forms or twice the frequency. The third harmonic or fifth tone, has three wave forms or thrice the frequency. To cover the whole fundamental octave of 12 notes, a sweep of 20 harmonics must be covered. Our ears tend to resolve all the harmonic frequency components, into a musical tone with an underlying timbre.

First harmonics:

Second harmonics:

And as the frequencies work together in harmony, so do His followers work together in harmony. (1 Peter 3:8-9) For each individual gives their own spirit, and works for the body of Christ, but the body works together in harmony, to glorify the Lord. But discordant tones can clash with the harmony, thus His believers are not to be bound with unbelievers. (2 Corinthians 6:14-15) And certain instruments like the cymbal, lack the attributes to produce a unified tone. Thus the Lord instructs us not to be clanging cymbals, "if I speak with the tongues of men and of angels, but do not have love, I have become a noisy gong or a clanging cymbal." (1 Corinthians 13:1).

Inharmonious & discordant:

Now that the end is near, the music will stop, and the heavens will be silenced, and the ***seven trumpets*** will sound. (Revelation 8:1-11:15) A trumpet is a brass instrument, with a cylindrical tube, that flares into a bell, and produces a resounding tone. The earliest trumpets were signaling instruments, utilized for military or religious purposes. And the typical range for a trumpet, is three octaves or ***seven*** overtones. And to trumpet symbolically means to sound a call of warning.

And the first trumpet was a warning, that the Lord was to punish His people, for their idolatry with the calf on Mount Sinai. (Exodus 19:18-20) And the Lord instructed Moses, to use the trumpet as a remembrance, whenever they went into battle. (Numbers 10:1-8) And the Lord instructed Joshua, to blow the trumpets for seven days, before the walls of Jericho would fall. (Joshua 6:3-7)

And the Judgment Day is upon us. For were we not warned by our forefathers, that the final trumpet would sound? (Psalms 98: 6-9) And did the prophets of old not promise, that the final trumpets would blow? (Joel 2:1-2) And did our LORD not forewarn us, that the trumpet would sound His return? (Matthew 24:30-31) And did Revelations not foretell, that the wrath and the fire would come? (Revelation 8:1-11:15) But the time is nigh and the Judgment Day looms, so make haste to make peace with the Lord. For when the final trumpet sounds, His forgiveness will be gone, and each must face on their own, the wrath and test of fire. But when all debts are paid in full, "the trumpet will sound, and the dead will be raised imperishable, and we will be changed. For this perishable must put on the imperishable, and this mortal must put on immortality." (1 Corinthians 15:51-53)

XVII

Christ the King Returns in Clouds (NASB)
To Andrew the Prophet
Completed October 11, 2007

"And then the sign of the Son of Man will appear in the sky, and then all the tribes of the earth will mourn, and they will see the SON OF MAN COMING ON THE **CLOUDS** OF THE SKY with power and great glory." Matthew 24:30

Clouds represent the Father's promise

"God said, 'This is the sign of the covenant which I am making between Me and you and every living creature that is with you, for all successive generations; I set My bow in the **cloud**, and it shall be for a sign of a covenant between Me and the earth.'" Genesis 9:12-13

"The LORD was going before them in a pillar of **cloud** by day to lead them on the way, and in a pillar of fire by night to give them light, that they might travel by day and by night. He did not take away the pillar of **cloud** by day, nor the pillar of fire by night, from before the people." Exodus 13:21-22

"And it came about, whenever Moses went out to the tent, that all the people would arise and stand, each at the entrance of his tent, and gaze after Moses until he entered the tent. Whenever Moses entered the tent, the pillar of **cloud** would descend and stand at the entrance of the tent; and the LORD would speak with Moses. When all the people saw the pillar of **cloud** standing at the entrance of the tent, all the people would arise and worship, each at the entrance of his tent." Exodus 33:8-11

"While he was still speaking, a bright **cloud** overshadowed them, and behold, a voice out of the **cloud** said, 'This is My beloved Son, with whom I am well-pleased; listen to Him!'" Matthew 9:13

God makes the clouds rain

"If the **cloud**s are full, they pour out rain upon the earth; and whether a tree falls toward the south or toward the north, wherever the tree falls, there it lies. He who watches the wind will not sow and he who looks at the **cloud**s will not reap." Ecclesiastes 11:3-4

"The waters saw You, O God; The waters saw You, they were in anguish; The deeps also trembled. The **cloud**s poured out water; The skies gave forth a sound; Your arrows flashed here and there. The sound of Your thunder was in the whirlwind; The lightnings lit up the world; The earth trembled and shook." Psalms 77:16-18

But in the judgment, the clouds will darken the skies and will rain hailstones and fire

"He made darkness His hiding place, His canopy around Him, Darkness of waters, thick **cloud**s of the skies. From the brightness before Him passed His thick **cloud**s, Hailstones and coals of fire. The LORD also thundered in the heavens, And the Most High uttered His voice, Hailstones and coals of fire." Psalms 18:11-13

"'And when I extinguish you, I will cover the heavens and darken their stars; I will cover the sun with a **cloud** And the moon will not give its light. All the shining lights in the heavens I will darken over you And will set darkness on your land,'Declares the Lord GOD" Ezekiel 32:7-8

"And the LORD will cause His voice of authority to be heard, And the descending of His arm to be seen in fierce anger, And in the flame of a consuming fire In **cloudburst**, downpour and hailstones." Isaiah 30:30

"I kept looking in the night visions, And behold, with the **cloud**s of given dominion, Glory and a kingdom, That all the peoples, nations and men of every language Might serve Him. His dominion is an everlasting dominion Which will not pass away; And His kingdom is one Which will not be destroyed." Daniel 7:13-14

"But immediately after the tribulation of those days THE SUN WILL BE DARKENED, AND THE MOON WILL NOT GIVE ITS LIGHT, AND THE STARS WILL FALL from the sky, and the powers of the heavens will be shaken. And then the sign of the Son of Man will appear in the sky, and then all the tribes of the earth will mourn, and they will see the SON OF MAN COMING ON THE **CLOUDS** OF THE SKY with power and great glory." Matthew 24:29

"And after He had said these things, He was lifted up while they were looking on, and a **cloud** received Him out of their sight. And as they were gazing intently into the sky while He was going, behold, two men in white clothing stood beside them. They also said, "Men of Galilee, why do you stand looking into the sky? This Jesus, who has been taken up from you into heaven, will come in just the same way as you have watched Him go into heaven." Acts 1:9-11

"And He was also saying to the crowds, "When you see a **cloud** rising in the west, immediately you say, 'A shower is coming,' and so it turns out. And when you see a south wind blowing, you say, 'It will be a hot day,' and it turns out that way. You hypocrites! You know how to analyze the appearance of the earth and the sky, but why do you not analyze this present time?" Luke 12:54-55

"For the Lord Himself will descend from heaven with a shout, with the voice of the archangel and with the trumpet of God, and the dead in Christ will rise first. Then we who are alive and remain will be caught up together with them in the **cloud**s to meet the Lord in the air, and so we shall always be with the Lord." 1 Thessalonians 4:16-17

"And they heard a loud voice from heaven saying to them, 'Come up here.' Then they went up into heaven in the **cloud**, and their enemies watched them...Then I looked, and behold, a white **cloud**, and sitting on the **cloud** was one like a son of man, having a golden crown on

103

His head and a sharp sickle in His hand. And another angel came out of the temple, crying out with a loud voice to Him who sat on the **cloud**, 'Put in your sickle and reap, for the hour to reap has come, because the harvest of the earth is ripe.' Then He who sat on the **cloud** swung His sickle over the earth, and the earth was reaped." Revelation 11:12-14:16

Christ the King Will Return on Clouds

"They will see the Son of Man coming on the clouds of the sky with power and great glory." (Matthew 24:29) The first covenant between God and man, was made in the clouds with the sun, and the last covenant will be made, when the Son returns on the clouds. And what was the first covenant of mankind? The clouds did rain and destroy mankind, but through the clouds God sent a sign, a rainbow as a promise to man, that He would not kill by rain again. (Genesis 9:12-13) And how were His people led through the desert? God led them with a pillar of cloud, as a reminder that He would dwell, with His people until the end. (Exodus 13:21-22) And from the entrance of the temple, God descended in a cloud, that He would speak to His people. (Exodus 33:8-11) And it is through the clouds, that the Father announced His only Son, "This is My beloved Son, with whom I am well-pleased; listen to Him!" (Matthew 9:13)

What is a cloud? A cloud is a visible body of water droplets suspended in the air. Symbolically, it is the suspended body of the Father (water) and the Spirit (air), and when the Son returns on the clouds, the Trinity shall be complete in the clouds.

And what makes a cloud form? Clouds are formed when water vapor condenses around a seed of water to form water droplets. And Christ sowed the good Seed of the Vine, for "He who sows the good seed is the Son of Man." (Matthew 13:37) And what makes the cloud precipitate? The winds cause the water droplets to collide, until they form raindrops which precipitate. And the wind of the Spirit intervenes through His children, to produce His fruits. For as the is everyone who is born of the Spirit." (John 3:8) For these are all conditions, which man cannot control, and even with our scientific advances, we still rely on God to rain on us, as He did on our forefathers. (Ecclesiastes 11:3-4) And we are constantly reminded, of the great devastation that rainstorms can cause. (Psalms 77:16-18) And the devastation rain can cause continues to this day.

But the end times are near. And no longer will it rain, but the clouds will darken the earth, and the skies will rain "hailstones and coals of fire".(Psalms 18:11-13) For did the prophets not foretell, that the land would be darkened by clouds? (Ezekiel 32:7-8) And that hailstones would fall from the skies? (Isaiah 30:30) And that the Son of Man would return on clouds? (Daniel 7:13-14) And did the Son not promise, that the sun and the moon would be darkened, and the stars would fall from the skies, and the Son of Man would return on clouds? (Matthew 24:29) And when the Lord ascended into the heavens, His angels promised that He would return, in the same way that He had risen. (Acts 1:9-11)

But woe to those who are left behind! For though mankind has learned, to read the signs in the skies, they do not recognize the signs that show, that the wrath is rapidly approaching. (Luke 12:54-55) For He promised that He would raise, His prophets and martyrs and saints, and then the wrath would ensue. (1 Thessalonians 4:16-17) And why will the skies be darkened? Because a nuclear holocaust shall occur, and according to nuclear experts, only three nuclear bombs are required, to cause the sunlight on the earth, to decrease to less than 5 percent. Yes and the kingdom shall be darkened! And why will it rain hailstones and coals of fire? After the nuclear explosion, tropospheric fallout particles will fall to the earth, from an hour to several days after the explosion. And these radioactive particles cause significant burn injuries, as well as carry very high amounts of radiation. Then as the atmosphere becomes heated, calcium carbonate and nitric oxide combine with rain to form acids (H_2SO_3 and HNO_3). In other words, the clouds will not rain water but will rain caustic organic acids! And finally, the seventh bowl of wrath is none other than a very large asteroid. "Then a strong angel took up a stone like a great millstone and threw it into the sea." (Revelation 18:21) And what will happen to all the debris, that is ejected into the atmosphere? "And huge hailstones, about one hundred pounds each, came down from heaven upon men; and men blasphemed God because of the plague of the hail, because its plague was extremely severe." (Revelation 16:21)

So make haste and recognize the signs in the clouds. For the Son of Man will return on the clouds, and He will harvest His firstfruits. (Revelation 11:12-14:16) And then the Day of Judgment will arrive, and woe to those who are not in the clouds!

XVIII

Faith is the Gold from God (NASB)
To Andrew the Prophet Completed
October 12, 2007

Gold was given to man as a gift

"Now a river flowed out of Eden to water the garden; and from there it divided and became four rivers. The name of the first is Pishon; it flows around the whole land of Havilah, where there is **gold**. The **gold** of that land is good; the bdellium and the onyx stone are there." Genesis 2:10-12

"They shall construct an ark of acacia wood two and a half cubits long, and one and a half cubits wide, and one and a half cubits high. You shall overlay it with pure **gold**, inside and out you shall overlay it, and you shall make a **gold** molding around it. You shall cast four **gold** rings for it and fasten them on its four feet, and two rings shall be on one side of it and two rings on the other side of it. You shall make poles of acacia wood and overlay them with **gold**." Exodus 25:10-13

"Solomon made all the furniture which was in the house of the LORD: the **golden** altar and the **golden** table on which was the bread of the Presence; and the lampstands, five on the right side and five on the left, in front of the inner sanctuary, of pure **gold**; and the flowers and the lamps and the tongs, of **gold**; and the cups and the snuffers and the bowls and the spoons and the firepans, of pure **gold**; and the hinges both for the doors of the inner house, the most holy place, and for the doors of the house, that is, of the nave, of **gold**. Thus all the work that King Solomon performed in the house of the LORD was finished. And Solomon brought in the things dedicated by his father David, the silver and the **gold** and the utensils, and he put them in the treasuries of the house of the LORD." 1 Kings 7:48-51

"The material of the wall was jasper; and the city was pure **gold**, like clear glass. The foundation stones of the city wall were adorned with every kind of precious stone...And the street of the city was pure **gold**, like transparent glass." Revelation 21:18-21

Gold can be a source of idolatry and greed

"You shall not make other gods besides Me; gods of silver or gods of **gold**, you shall not make for yourselves." Exodus 20:23

"He shall not multiply wives for himself, or else his heart will turn away; nor shall he greatly increase silver and **gold** for himself." Deuteronomy 17:17

"For they said to me, 'Make a god for us who will go before us; for this Moses, the man who brought us up from the land of Egypt, we do not know what has become of him.' I said to them, 'Whoever has any **gold**, let them tear it off.' So they gave it to me, and I threw it into the fire, and out came this calf." Exodus 23:24

"Now the weight of gold which came in to Solomon in one year was *666* talents of **gold**" 1 Kings 10:14

"Those who lavish **gold** from the purse And weigh silver on the scale Hire a goldsmith, and he makes it into a god; They bow down, indeed they worship it. They lift it upon the shoulder and carry it; They set it in its place and it stands there. It does not move from its place. Though one may cry to it, it cannot answer; It cannot deliver him from his distress." Isaiah 46:6-7

"Come now, you rich, weep and howl for your miseries which are coming upon you. Your riches have rotted and your garments have become moth-eaten. Your **gold** and your silver have rusted; and their rust will be a witness against you and will consume your flesh like fire. It is in the last days that you have stored up your treasure." James 5:1-3

And in the end gold will be destroyed

"Remember Him before the silver cord is broken and the **golden** bowl is crushed, the pitcher by the well is shattered and the wheel at the cistern is crushed; then the dust will return to the earth as it was, and the spirit will return to God who gave it." Ecclesiastes 12:6-7

"I will make mortal man scarcer than pure **gold** And mankind than the **gold** of Ophir. Therefore I will make the heavens tremble, And the earth will be shaken from its place At the fury of the LORD of hosts In the day of His burning anger." Isaiah 13:12-13

But Christ came and gave us His Gold which His faithfulness

"The young camels of Midian and Ephah; All those from Sheba will come; They will bring **gold** and frankincense, And will bear good news of the praises of the LORD." Isaiah 60:5-6

"After coming into the house they saw the Child with Mary His mother; and they fell to the ground and worshiped Him. Then, opening their treasures, they presented to Him gifts of **gold**, frankincense, and myrrh." Matthew 2:11

"I lifted my eyes and looked, and behold, there was a certain man dressed in linen, whose waist was girded with a belt of pure **gold** of Uphaz." Daniel 10:5

"Also righteousness will be the belt about His loins, And **faithfulness** the belt about His waist" Isaiah 11:5

The Gold of Faith is a Gift from God

"Enter His gates with thanksgiving And His courts with praise. Give thanks to Him, bless His name. For the LORD is good; His lovingkindness is everlasting And His **faithfulness** to all generations" Psalms 100:4-5

"Kings will see and arise, Princes will also bow down, Because of the LORD who is **faithful**, the Holy One of Israel who has chosen You." Isaiah 49:7

"But if God so clothes the grass of the field, which is alive today and tomorrow is thrown into the furnace, will He not much more clothe you? You of little **faith**! ... But seek first His kingdom and His righteousness, and all these things will be added to you." Matthew 6:30-33

"For by grace you have been saved through **faith**; and that not of yourselves, it is the gift of God" Ephesians 2:8

"In this you greatly rejoice, even though now for a little while, if necessary, you have been distressed by various trials, so that the proof of your **faith**, being more precious than **gold** which is perishable, even though tested by fire, may be found to result in praise and glory and honor at the revelation of Jesus Christ." 1 Peter 1:6-7

Our Faith in God comes at great cost

"Now that no one is justified by the Law before God is evident; for, 'THE RIGHTEOUS MAN SHALL LIVE BY **FAITH**.;" Galatians 3:11

"But now that **faith** has come, we are no longer under a tutor. For you are all sons of God through faith in Christ Jesus." Galatians 3:25

"What use is it, my brethren, if someone says he has **faith** but he has no works? Can that **faith** save him?...For just as the body without the spirit is dead, so also **faith** without works is dead." James 2:14-26

"Now **faith** is the assurance of things hoped for, the conviction of things not seen... They were stoned, they were sawn in two, they were tempted, they were put to death with the sword; they went about in sheepskins, in goatskins, being destitute, afflicted, ill-treated men of whom the world was not worthy, wandering in deserts and mountains and caves and holes in the ground. And all these, having gained approval through their **faith**, did not receive what was promised, because God had provided something better for us, so that apart from us they would not be made perfect." Hebrews 11:1-37

And our gold will be tested in the furnace

"And I will bring the third part through the fire, Refine them as silver is refined, And test them as **gold** is tested. They will call on My name, And I will answer them; I will say, 'They are My people,' And they will say, 'The LORD is my God.'" Zechariah 13:9

"Now if any man builds on the foundation with **gold**, silver, precious stones, wood, hay, straw, each man's work will become evident; for the day will show it because it is to be revealed with fire, and the fire itself will test the quality of each man's work. If any man's work which he has built on it remains, he will receive a reward. If any man's work is burned up, he will suffer loss; but he himself will be saved, yet so as through fire." 1 Corinthians 3:12-15

"The King's daughter is all glorious within; Her clothing is interwoven with **gold**. She will be led to the King in embroidered work; The virgins, her companions who follow her, Will be brought to You. They will be led forth with gladness and rejoicing; They will enter into the King's palace." Psalms 45:13-15

"When He had taken the book, the four living creatures and the twenty-four elders fell down before the Lamb, each one holding a harp and **golden** bowls full of incense, which are the prayers of the saints." Revelation 5:8

"Here is the perseverance of the saints who keep the commandments of God and their **faith** in Jesus. And I heard a voice from heaven, saying, 'Write, 'Blessed are the dead who die in the Lord from now on!''' Yes,' says the Spirit, 'so that they may rest from their labors, for their deeds follow with them.'" Revelation 14:12-13

"And I saw heaven opened, and behold, a white horse, and He who sat on it is called **Faithful** and True, and in righteousness He judges and wages war... And on His robe and on His thigh He has a name written, "KING OF KINGS, AND LORD OF LORDS."" Revelation 19:11-16

Faith is God's Gold

Gold is a soft corrosion-resistant element, and is the most malleable metal on earth. Because of its beauty and its malleable nature, it is used for currency, jewelry, and decoration. It is also used as a term, to denote something of great value or goodness. (*i.e. a heart of gold.*) Its chemical symbol is *Au,* derived from the Latin word *aurum,* which in translation means glowing dawn.

From the dawn of mankind at the rivers of Eden, God blessed the earth with a wealth of gold. (Genesis 2:10-12) And from that gold Moses was told, to enclose God's covenant in an ark of gold. (Exodus 25:10-13) And from that gold God instructed Solomon, to construct His temple of gold. (1 Kings 7:48-51) And the magnificence of the golden temple, was a glimpse of the glory of the kingdom to come. (Revelation 21:18-21)

But with any wealth comes idolatry and greed. And from His covenant God told His people, not to construct any idols of gold. (Exodus 20:23) And He warned them not to hoard their gold. (Deuteronomy 17:17) But what did they do? While Moses was receiving the covenant from God, His people transgressed in sin and idolatry, and constructed and worshiped a calf of gold. (Exodus 23:24) And the people in idolatry and greed, would hoard their gold and make it their god. (Isaiah 46:6-7) And the amount of gold received in the coffer (666), would foretell of the curse of its perils. (1 Kings 10:14) For the day will come when their gold will rust, and it will be a witness against them, and it will consume their flesh like fire. (James 5:1-3)

And why do we place such value, in the material things of this world? And why do we worship like gold, the treasures of this world, but not the treasures of God? For Solomon warned that all things on earth would return to the earth, and that all things of the Father would return to the Father. And our bodies will return to the earth, and our souls will return to the Father. (Ecclesiastes 12:6-7) For the body will burn with the earth, and the body of man will be scarcer than gold. (Isaiah 13:12-13)

What is the ancient symbol for gold? (•) It is the ancient symbol for the Sun God. And God in His mercy promised His people, that His Son would come to the earth, to bring the true Gold of God. (Isaiah 60:5-6) And in Bethlehem the prophecy was fulfilled. (Matthew 2:11) For the prophets foretold that the Son would come, with a belt of pure gold about His waist.(Daniel 10:5) And His belt was not gold of the earth, but a belt of God's faithfulness to man. (Isaiah 11:5) For God in His faithfulness sent us His Son, that all men may be saved.

But why do we boast, that we have such great faith? The psalmist did not give praise for our faithfulness, but for God's faithfulness to all generations. (Psalms 100:4-5) And the prophets of old foretold, that the princes of earth would bow down, because of His faithfulness to man. (Isaiah 49:7) And Christ promised by His faithfulness, that He would return for all men. For He taught of God's faithfulness to man, and gave us great faith in His kingdom to come. (Matthew 6:30-31) And each has been given some faith, according to God's own good pleasure, and not out of any merit of our own, for our faith "is the gift of God".(Ephesians 2:8) And Peter said the gift of faith is more precious than gold, for at His return, our faith in Him will be redeemed with glory and honor. (1 Peter 1:6-7)

Although our faith is a gift from God, it comes at a very great price. For the true fruit of faith is our righteousness. (Galatians 3:11) And what is righteousness? It is believing in God regardless of the circumstance!   For God committed Abraham to sacrifice His son, and "Abraham believed God, and it was credited to him as righteousness." (Romans 4:3) For when we receive the gift of faith, we become like the Son of God, for we become sons of the Father. (Galatians 3:25) But just as Christ accomplished great works, so must we complete the works of the Spirit. (James 2:14-26) For as gold can produce great works of from our hands, so can faith produce great works of the Spirit. And just as Christ suffered greatly for His faithfulness, so must we suffer greatly for our faith. But through these trials our faith is perfected, and the promise of the rewards will come, for the time of redemption is soon. (Hebrews 11:1-37)

And how is gold refined and tested? It is refined and tested with fire. For the Lord has refined His people, with the trials of this earthly existence, and they will be tested by the fire, and the Lord "will say, 'They are My people,' And they will say, 'The LORD is my God.'" (Zechariah 13:9) And on that day man's gold will be tested; and the question will be,... is your gold the perishable gold of the earth, or the imperishable gold of God's faith and righteousness? (1 Corinthians 3:12-15) And the rewards will be great for the bride, (the prophets, martyrs, and saints) for "they will enter into the King's palace." (Psalms 45:13-15) And when they have entered the palace, they (the creature with four heads) will bow down to the King, and their prayers will be heard in the heavens. (Revelation 5:8) And their prayers will be for the glory of the King, and the salvation of all of mankind.

But for those with the perishable gold of this earth, all will be lost, for the fire will test each man's works. For "if any man's work is burned up, he will suffer loss; but he himself will be saved, yet so as through fire." (1 Corinthians 3:15) For by His good grace, after each debt is paid, all will be redeemed according to their gold, and all will enter His kingdom of gold. (Revelation 14:12-13) And when the last bowl has been poured, the One who is "Faithful and True", will defeat Satan and death, for He is the Lamb and the Lion, for He is the "KING OF KINGS, AND LORD OF LORDS." (Revelation 19:11-16)

XIX

Oil Anoints Before the Fire (NASB)
To Andrew the Prophet Completed
October 15, 2007

"A quart of wheat for a denarius, and three quarts of barley for a denarius; and do not damage the **oil** and the wine." Revelation 6:5-6

Oil keeps the lamp lit for His return

"You shall charge the sons of Israel, that they bring you clear **oil** of beaten olives for the light, to make a lamp burn continually. In the tent of meeting, outside the veil which is before the testimony, Aaron and his sons shall keep it in order from evening to morning before the LORD; it shall be a perpetual statute throughout their generations for the sons of Israel." Exodus 27:20-21

"Then the kingdom of heaven will be comparable to ten virgins, who took their lamps and went out to meet the bridegroom. Five of them were foolish, and five were prudent. For when the foolish took their lamps, they took no **oil** with them, but the prudent took **oil** in flasks along with their lamps. Now while the bridegroom was delaying, they all got drowsy and began to sleep. But at midnight there was a shout, 'Behold, the bridegroom! Come out to meet him. Then all those virgins rose and trimmed their lamps. The foolish said to the prudent, 'Give us some of your **oil**, for our lamps are going out.' But the prudent answered, 'No, there will not be enough for us and you too; go instead to the dealers and buy some for yourselves.' And while they were going away to make the purchase, the bridegroom came, and those who were ready went in with him to the wedding feast; and the door was shut. 'Later the other virgins also came, saying, 'Lord, lord, open up for us.' But he answered, 'Truly I say to you, I do not know you.'" Matthew 25:1-12

God promised us His oil

"It shall come about, if you listen obediently to my commandments which I am commanding you today, to love the LORD your God and to serve Him with all your heart and all your soul, that He will give the rain for your land in its season, the early and late rain, that you may gather in your grain and your new wine and your **oil**." Deuteronomy 11:13-14

"For thus says the LORD God of Israel, 'The bowl of flour shall not be exhausted, nor shall the jar of **oil** be empty, until the day that the LORD sends rain on the face of the earth.'" 1 Kings 17:14

"The LORD will answer and say to His people, 'Behold, I am going to send you grain, new wine and **oil**, And you will be satisfied in full with them; And I will never again make you a reproach among the nations. But I will remove the northern army far from you, And I will drive it into a parched and desolate land, And its vanguard into the eastern sea, And its rear guard into the western sea. And its stench will arise and its foul smell will come up, For it has done great things.'" Joel 2:19-20

Oil anoints the guilt offering

"Then the priest shall take the one male lamb and bring it for a guilt offering, with the log of **oil**, and present them as a wave offering before the LORD. Next he shall slaughter the male lamb in the place where they slaughter the sin offering and the burnt offering, at the place of the sanctuary--for the guilt offering, like the sin offering, belongs to the priest; it is most holy...The priest shall then put some of the **oil** that is in his palm on the lobe of the right ear of the one to be cleansed, and on the thumb of his right hand and on the big toe of his right foot, on the place of the blood of the guilt offering. Moreover, the rest of the **oil** that is in the priest's palm he shall put on the head of the one to be cleansed, to make atonement on his behalf before the LORD." Leviticus 14:12-29

"Even though I walk through the valley of the shadow of death, I fear no evil, for You are with me; Your rod and Your staff, they comfort me. You prepare a table before me in the presence of my enemies; You have anointed my head with **oil**; My cup overflows. Surely goodness and lovingkindness will follow me all the days of my life, And I will dwell in the house of the LORD forever." Psalms 23:4-6

"And when Jesus was in Bethany at the house of Simon the leper, a woman came to Him having an alabaster flask of very costly fragrant **oil**, and she poured it on His head as He sat at the table. But when His disciples saw it, they were indignant, saying, 'To what purpose is this waste? For this fragrant **oil** might have been sold for much and given to the poor.' But when Jesus was aware of it, He said to them, "Why do you trouble the woman? For she has done a good work for Me. For you have the poor with you always, but Me you do not have always. For in pouring this fragrant **oil** on My body, she did it for My burial." Matthew 26:6-12

Oil also comes from the earth

"The LORD alone guided him, And there was no foreign god with him. He made him ride on the high places of the earth, And he ate the produce of the field; And He made him suck honey from the rock, And **oil** from the flinty rock" Deuteronomy 32:12-13

"For the lips of an adulteress drip honey And smoother than **oil** is her speech; But in the end she is bitter as wormwood, Sharp as a two-edged sword. Her feet go down to death, Her steps take hold of Sheol." Proverbs 5:3-5

"He who loves pleasure will become a poor man; He who loves wine and **oil** will not become rich." Proverbs 21:16

But mankind refused the Oil of atonement

"You will sow but you will not reap. You will tread the olive but will not anoint yourself with **oil**; And the grapes, but you will not drink wine. The statutes of Omri And all the works of the house of Ahab are observed; And in their devices you walk. Therefore I will give you up for destruction And your inhabitants for derision, And you will bear the reproach of My people." Micah 6:15-16

"The field is ruined, The land mourns; For the grain is ruined, The new wine dries up, Fresh **oil** fails. Be ashamed, O farmers, Wail, O vinedressers, For the wheat and the barley; Because the harvest of the field is destroyed. The vine dries up And the fig tree fails; The pomegranate, the palm also, and the apple tree, All the trees of the field dry up. Indeed, rejoicing dries up From the sons of men." Joel 1:10-12

"When He broke the third seal, I heard the third living creature saying, 'Come.' I looked, and behold, a black horse; and he who sat on it had a pair of scales in his hand. And I heard something like a voice in the center of the four living creatures saying, 'A quart of wheat for a denarius, and three quarts of barley for a denarius; and do not damage the **oil** and the wine.'" Revelation 6:5-6

The Oil of Atonement or the Oil of Destruction

Oil is a substance derived from animals, vegetables, and minerals, which has a slippery viscous and often flammable property. It does not mix well with water, due to its hydrophobic or "water-fearing" properties. The first oil products were derived from the olive tree, over 3000 years before Christ. The olive oil was used in the temple of God, to anoint the guilt offerings and keep the lamps lit. However Big Oil or "Oil" for short, refers to the economic and political power, of the oil companies, executives, and their owners. A slang term for oil is insincere flattery, intended to bribe an authority, something that "Oil" is well accustomed to. Oil is important at these end times, because of the beast from the sea. For Satan has sent for his sons of perdition, whose love for oil shall burn with this earth.

Oil is extracted from olive trees, as a means to supply lamps with light. For the Lord told Moses to keep, the seven lamps of the temple lit with its oil. (Exodus 27:20-21) And when the Lord returns, the prophets, martyrs, and saints will be the reconstructed temple of God, and the seven lamp stands will stand before the Son of Man. "Then I turned to see the voice that spoke with me. And having turned I saw seven golden lampstands, and in the midst of the seven lampstands One like the Son of Man, clothed with a garment down to the feet and girded about the chest with a golden band." (Revelation 1:12) And the seven lamp stands will pour, the oil of God's wrath on the earth, for the seven lamp stands are the seven angels of wrath. " Then I saw another sign in heaven, great and marvelous: seven angels having the seven last plagues, for in them the wrath of God is complete." (Revelation 15:1)

And what does it mean to have a lamp? It means to be light. For the Lord called on His people, to be the light of the world. For He came to this world to be Light, but the Light could not stay, for the Light had to die, that we could be saved. But by His resurrection, He gave us the Holy Spirit. And through the Holy Spirit, He called on His children to be light of the world, that the whole world would know, of His Word and His sacrifice, and glorify the Father in heaven. "You are the light of the world. A city that is set on a hill cannot be hidden. Nor do they light a lamp and put it under a basket, but on a lampstand, and it gives light to all who are in the house. Let your light so shine before men, that they may see your good works and glorify your Father in heaven." (Matthew 5:14-16)

And how do we keep our lamps lit? With the oil of readiness. For the Lord had warned to keep our lamps lit, for the day of judgment would come, like a thief in the night. And the bride of the Groom will be ready, but the world will not be ready for that day, for the oil in their lamps will be dry. "And while they were going away to make the purchase, the bridegroom came, and those who were ready went in with him to the wedding feast; and the door was shut. Later the other virgins also came, saying, 'Lord, lord, open up for us.' But he answered, 'Truly I say to you, I do not know you.'" (Matthew 25:1-12) And the way to be ready is to keep our lamps lit, to rely on the Father, to know the Lord's Words, to accept His forgiveness, and to produce the works of the Spirit.

And the Lord promised that He would give us the oil, if we obeyed His commands. (Deuteronomy 11:13-14) And He promised that we would have oil to keep our lamps lit for that day. (1 Kings 17:14) And He promised to us on that day, that His faithful will inherit the Light, for their lamps will no longer need oil, because they will dwell with the Light of the Lord. (Joel 2:19-20)

What else is oil used for? Oil is used to anoint the guilt offering. For Aaron was commanded by God, to anoint the guilt offering of the lamb, as an atonement for the sins of His people. (Leviticus 14:12-29) And the psalmist reminds of God's mercy and grace, "You have anointed my head with oil; My cup overflows. Surely goodness and lovingkindness will follow me all the days of my life, And I will dwell in the house of the LORD forever." (Psalms 23:4-6) And by the grace of God, He sent His only Son to be the Lamb of God, to be the guilt offering for the sins of the world. And before He was crucified, He was anointed with oil, to prepare for His death and His burial. (Matthew 26:6-12) And by His death on the cross, He became an atonement, for those who would call on name of the Lamb.

Where else does oil come from? Oil is derived from the minerals of the earth. And the Lord instructed His people, to use the oil from the rock, as a healing ointment for their ailments. (Deuteronomy 32:12-13) But though a source of heat and light, this oil was not used for the offering. For this oil is hydrophobic because it repels water. And those who have fornicated with oil, by the deceit of the Bush staff and Big Oil, are repulsive to God the Father (water). For their oil is the speech of an adulteress, with smooth words that lead down to Sheol. (Proverbs 5:3-5) And the oil from the earth has been fornicated, by deceitful and murderous lies. They will burn with their oil in the wrath. And irony of ironies! Solomon foretold that their justice would come! "He who loves wine and **oil** will not become rich." (Proverbs 21:16)

Man has refused the oil of the olive, and the oil of atonement from God. And in just recompense they shall receive, the fire and wrath of His judgment. (Micah 6:15-16) For the oil of atonement is imperishable, but mankind has turned to the oil of the earth. For this oil will burn in the fire, when the Lord returns as the Lion. And the Lion is **No OIL** in reverse. For they will have **No OIL** for atonement and **No OIL** for their lamps. For the oil of the earth will fail, and the fruits of the harvest will die, and the vine will dry out, and their rejoicing will turn into mourning. (Joel 1:10-12) For when the 3rd seal is broken, in July of 2009, Uganda will suffer from a famine, but the world will be blind as the signs are unfolding. And man will continue to hoard their oil, but the Lord will save the wine, and on that Day the wrath will come. But "do not damage the **oil** and the **wine**". (Revelation 6:5-6) For the "OIL" will burn and bleed in the fire!

X X

Oil-Currency: Trading for the €nd (NASB)
To Andrew the Prophet
Completed October 16, 2007

"A quart of wheat for a denarius, and three quarts of barley for a denarius; and do not damage the **oil** and the wine." Revelation **6:6**

"And he causes all, the small and the great, and the rich and the poor, and the free men and the slaves, to be given a mark on their right hand or on their forehead, and he provides that no one will be able to buy or to sell, except the one who has the mark, either the name of the beast or the number of his name." Revelation 13:16-17

Oil-currency is the exchange rate for the end times

The end times were put into motion over a century ago when <u>oil</u> became a major means of influencing the world's currency. For prior to that, the major means of influencing the world's currency was through <u>war</u>. And now the world powers have two means of influencing the world's economy. And what is the world's major currency? It is still the US dollar, which accounts for two thirds of all of the world's exchange reserves. More than 80% of all foreign exchange transactions and over 50% of all world imports are exchanged in US dollars.

Because the world exchange currency is in US dollars, our government and nation can essentially produce paper currency and receive imports at almost no cost. Our US dollar has little equitable

122

financial backing, except for the fact that it is the currency by which foreign trade is conducted. This is reflected in the fact that the value of our imports greatly exceeds the value of our exports. In fact just last year, the economic value of our imports was worth more than 50% of our export value.

The major objective of bringing the Euro (€ **for end times**) into the market was to turn the Euro into a reserve currency in order to compete against the US dollar. And a major means of allowing other countries to compete against the US dollar was the ability for them to convert the exchange currency of oil from US dollars to Euros. By forcing oil currency into Euros, the US (the #1 importer of oil) would be forced to exchange US dollars into Euros, and due to the loss of exchange value, this would cause a domino effect on the trade value of the US dollar. Conservative estimates suggest that a conversion to Euros would decrease the dollar value by more than 40%. Ultimately, this would lead to a major crash of the US property and stock markets, thus spiraling the US into a major recession.

And in fact, in November 2000, Saddam Hussein decided to attack the US economy in retaliation for Desert Storm and subsequent trade embargos, by converting Iraq's oil exchange into Euros. This caused a significant decrease in the US dollar exchange rate, and OPEC (the Organization of Petroleum Exporting Countries) was threatening to follow in suit. Because we could not control a regime like Iraq economically, our government decided to use alternative means to control their oil currency,..**military force**. Presently, Iran has also converted its oil exchange to the Euro to show support from the "longer horn" (Iran) to the "shorter horn" (Iraq). And historically, this relationship will go down in infamy. "Now the two horns (Iraq & Iran) were long, but one (Mahmoud Ahmadinejad) was longer than the other (Moqtada al-Sadr), with the longer one coming up last" (Daniel 8:3)

†Notation on ε: **Epsilon** is the fifth letter of the Greek alphabet. Interestingly, in mathematics, it means a small quantity of anything. i.e. "The cost is only epsilon" And the Euro was introduced into

the market because the US was purchasing oil for just an "epsilon" amount. And ε is also utilized in economics as a measurement called elasticity. Elasticity measures how much the demand of a product changes as its price changes. For example, oil economically has a low elasticity, because the economy requires oil regardless of its price. And due to oil's low elasticity, the oil industry can increase the price of oil or increase their profit margin at will, because the public always has a high demand for its product. And in fact in 2005, the US oil industry had revenues in excess of 1.6 trillion dollars, and over 80% of the revenue was accounted for by the major oil companies or "Big Oil".

Oil-currency is the reason for military and economic force

For those of you who doubt the effect that **oil** has on the world and what seductive powers it has over our leaders, here is a brief history lesson:

Oil is required for almost every aspect of our economic and military power. It is required for transportation (land, sea, and air), heating, agriculture, medications, machinery, and synthetic manufacturing i.e. plastics and rubber. Moreover, oil use has sky rocketed over the past century because of gas-guzzling automobiles, neglect of public transportation, dispersed suburban housing patterns, and the excessive consumption of products. At present, the world is consuming 80 million barrels of oil daily. The US is presently the number one consumer and importer of oil at a consumption rate of about 20 million barrels daily. Each US citizen consumes about 1 barrel of oil every 2 weeks. Due to the poverty of the Middle East region, foreign oil has always been much cheaper to produce and transport than domestic oil, thus giving the oil companies a huge profit margin and the incentive to obtain oil overseas rather than domestically. The US government has tried in the past to control oil supplies independently, but due to the opposition of the private sector, it has never been able to do so. Because of that, the government is largely controlled by the interests of the private oil companies, most notably the Seven Sisters: Exxon, Mobil, Chevron, Texaco, Gulf Oil, British Petroleum, and Shell. Of principle concern to these companies, is maintaining the security and stability of the Middle Eastern region. As we know, this has often entailed using covert and blatantly militaristic schemes to ensure control of certain countries, namely Iraq, Iran, Afghanistan and Kuwait. And now that the US has military control of Iraq and Afghanistan, we now have control of 75% of the world oil reserves (i.e. **one-hundred thousand barrels daily** from Caspian reserves via the trans-Afghanistan pipeline and **two-hundred-fifty billion** barrels of Iraqi oil). Clearly, the US hopes to control world oil trade and force opposing nations to purchase oil in US dollars rather than Euros, and thus force nations to hold hundreds of billions of US dollars in reserve for future transactions.

A BRIEF HISTORY LESSON IN OIL

M = military   ε = economic   Highlights nvolve the Middle East

1886   ε   Gas powered automobile invented

1890   ε   US overtakes Great Britain as the major industrial power of the world

1901   ε   Massive oil fields found in Texas

1909   ε   Model T introduced by Ford, drives demand for oil

1914   M   World War I - usage of oil causes massive shortage, thus future military and economic efforts are geared towards securing oil reserves

1920   ε   Oil becomes the fuel of choice for land (automobiles), sea, and air transportation

      ε   Oil becomes critical for agriculture (pesticides and fertilizers)

      ε   US becomes the number one oil exporter and Britain and France rely on the US for oil supplies ε Open door policy for private US oil companies (not the US government) to access foreign oil

ε Agreements between British and US oil companies to allocate, fix prices, and monopolize oil

ε Mexican dictator Diaz exports oil to the US

ε **US & European oil companies begin drilling for Middle Eastern Oil**

1928 ε **Iraq Petroleum Company established - allows select US oil companies access to Iraqi oil**

1930 ε Discovery of the great East Texas oil field

ε Germany relies on the Soviet Union for oil supplies

ε Japan relies on the US for oil supplies

ε US switches imports from Mexico to Venezuela due to concern over the Mexican Revolution

ε Defeat of the Anglo-American Oil Agreement which would have allowed domestic oil to compete fairly with foreign oil imports

1930 ε **Standard Oil of California (SOCAL) - now Chevron - controls oil in Bahrain off Saudi Arabia**

1933 ε **The Texas Company, now Texaco, and SOCAL have oil concession rights in Saudi Arabia**

1935 ε Dupont invents nylon which is derived from oil products

1936 ε **The Gulf Oil Company has oil concession rights in Kuwait**

1938 ε Mexican nationalization, takes over oil production in the Gulf of Mexico, US boycotts Mexican oil

1940 ε **Roosevelt attempts to set up a government owned oil company to take oil rights in Saudi Arabia. However, private oil companies oppose government control, and the proposal for a government controlled oil company is abandoned.**

ε Huge tax breaks for oil companies to import foreign oil

1941 M Germany attacks Soviet Union to take over Russian oil fields

M Japan attacks US (Pearl Harbor) to assume control of the Netherlands East Indies oil fields (Japan decimates the US Pacific armada which protects this region)

M US supplies oil for the war effort and its European allies, which causes a strain on US oil reserves

1944 M US regains control of the Pacific, Japan's military crippled by oil shortage

M Soviets regain control of oil fields, Germany's military crippled by oil shortage

1946 ε **"Great oil deals" - US oil companies secure control of Middle East oil mediated by Roosevelt**

1947 M Truman Doctrine - US committed to global containment of communism

1948 M Military coup in Venezuela, US continues to work with Venezuelan dictatorship for oil

M **US supports Israeli independence causing alienation from Middle East suppliers; however, the private oil companies distance themselves from the US government and maintain a relationship with the Middle East**

1950 ε Oil is responsible for 29% of the world energy consumption ε US oil companies dominate the oil-producing regions outside of the Soviet Union

ε US supplies oil to Germany and Japan to spur growth & control recurrence of nationalistic aggression

ε US supplies oil to Western Europe to control Soviet aggression

ε Seven Sisters control 90% of the oil reserves and 75% of the refineries in the world

ε Soviet oil production drops drastically and shut out from oil imports from the Middle East

ε Oil prices drop due to competition and oversupply of oil

1951 ε **Iranian nationalization under Massadeq takes over British owned oil companies, Britain calls for an international boycott of Iranian oil, Iran positioned to become a <u>DEMOCRATIC</u> nation**

ε Phillips Petroleum develops plastics, derived from oil products

1953 M **US and Britain organize, finance, and direct a coup against Massadeq and establish a pro-US government under the dictatorship of the Shah of Iran, US oil companies take over control of Iranian oil**

1954 ε Alternative fuel energy program abandoned by Eisenhower due to pressure from private oil companies

1958 M **US attacks Lebanon to set up a pro-US regime**

M **Brigadier Qassem takes over the British installed king of Iraq, becomes a communist tolerant state**

1956 M **Suez crisis: Egyptian nationalist Nasser takes over Suez canal (2/3 of oil from the Middle East to Western Europe travels through the canal), US refuses to** assist British and French to pressure Egypt into relinquishing control of the Suez, US rather than Europe becomes the controlling foreign power in the Middle East region

1960 ε **OPEC (Organization of the Petroleum Exporting Countries) is formed in Baghdad - oil ministers in Iran, Iraq, Kuwait, Saudi Arabia, and Venezuela coalesce to control oil market prices**

M **Ayatollah Khomeini expelled from Iran, lives in exile in Iraq under protection of al-Sadr**

1963 M **Iraq's Qassem overthrown by CIA backed coup, Iraq power assumed by Ba'ath party (Saddam Hussein's party)**

1967 M **Arab-Israeli Six Day War, US support of Israel causes a strain on US-Arab relations, OPEC raises oil prices 70 percent and embargos US oil shipments, Iraq-US relations severed**

ε **Nationalization of Iraqi oil, control is transferred to the Iraq National Oil Company**

1969 M **Nixon announces the US will rely on and support regional allies, Iran and Saudi Arabia.**

This results in the US trade of the latest military equipment to the Middle East countries.

1970 ε Oil is responsible for 46% of world energy consumption (47% of US energy consumption, 80% of Japan's energy consumption, 64% of Europe's energy consumption)

ε US produces only 20% of worlds oil production

ε Oil imports rise from 9% in the 1950s to 36% to meet US oil consumption ε Middle East accounts for more than 40% of the world's oil production

ε OPEC countries nationalize their oil industries; however, the Seven Sisters receive a huge compensation and maintain their oil access to the Middle East

1972 M Saddam Hussein signs Iraqi-Soviet Friendship Treaty causing US to shift away from Iraqi oil

M Nixon sells $22 billion in arms sales to the Shah of Iran, US sends military support to Kurds in Northern Iraq

1973 M Israel-Palestinian Yom-Kippur war, US alienates Middle Eastern countries due to assistance

ε OPEC embargos against the US cause oil shock and severe economic recession

1974 ε IEA (International Energy Agency) established - Western nations organize to reduce future reliance on Middle East oil

1979 M Iranian revolution, the US friendly Shah is overtaken by Ayatollah Khomeini, establishes the *Islamic fundamentalist government* of present day Iran, results in oil shortage in the US

ε Iranian oil shortage causes an increase in inflation, unemployment, and interest rates in the US

M Iran-US hostage situation, Iran-Contra negotiations through Reagan and Bush, Sr.

M Saddam Hussein assumes control of Iraq, due to loss of control in Iran, US shifts military support to Iraq

1980 M Carter doctrine: sets up rapid deployment forces for use of military force in the Middle East. US sells sophisticated military arms and US treasury securities to Saudi Arabia

M Iran-Iraq War: US supplies Saddam Hussein in Iraq with military weapons

M US gives military assistance to Osama bin Laden to fight against the Soviets in Afghanistan, US assistance helps in forming the present day al-Qaeda

1981 M Reagan transforms the Rapid Deployment Force into the Central Command

1984 M Increased US military support given to Saddam Hussein to oppose Iran

1986 ε Oil prices collapse due to increased supply and decreased demand

ε Soviet Union suffers greatly due to collapse of oil earnings, eventually leads to collapse of the Iron Wall

1988 M Saddam Hussein attacks Iranian troops in Northern Iraq, US increases military support

1990 ε US imports 25% of oil from the Middle East

ε Gas prices remain low, energy consumption increases drastically

M Iraq invades Kuwait to assume control of their oil fields

1991 M Operation Desert Storm: 200,000 Iraqi troops killed

M Hussein withdraws troops from Kuwait, sets fire to oil wells

M Embargos against Iraq following Desert Storm results in deaths of 1 million children due to lack of water, medications, and starvation ε   Iron Wall collapses due to economic collapse of Soviet Union

1998 ε   Oil prices drop to $10 per barrel, causes surge in energy consumption

2000 ε   **Sharp increases in oil prices due to rising consumption and OPEC production cuts**

2000 ε   **Iraq becomes first OPEC nation to trade oil for Euros**

2001 M **Al-Qaeda under Osama bin Laden attacks the US: NY Trade Towers**

     M **Afghanistan war: US establishes new regime in Afghanistan, US builds one-million barrel/day Afghanistan oil pipeline**

2002 M **Massive air strikes on Iraqi targets occurs one month prior to US Congress giving Bush the authority to invade**

     M **Bush administration claims Iraq has Weapons of Mass Destruction (WMD)**

     M **UN and International Atomic Energy Agency find <u>no evidence of WMD</u> prior to US-Iraq War**

2003 M **Iraq War - also considered by Jihadists to be the final holy war, WW 3**

     M **No Weapons of Mass Destruction found**

     ε   **Lucrative multibillion dollar contracts offered to <u>Halliburton</u> (<u>Kellogg Brown and Root</u> - a subsidiary of Halliburton ($18.5 billion contract), and <u>Bechtel</u> - multiple connections to White House under Bush Sr.**

2005 M **Iraq approaches civil war**

2007   M 3830 US troops killed; 27,753 US troops injured; 1,087,731 Iraqi civilians killed as of October 2007

ε Cost of war $470 billion as of October 2007

BUSH ADMINISTRATION

And perhaps there is a conflict of interest in the present US White House administration. Here are their credentials:

Dick Cheney, Vice President:

1995-2000: President of Halliburton, Close ties to Shell and Chevron

1992 Halliburton $8 billion contract to put out Kuwait oil fires

2001 Cheney organizes Energy Task Force - advisors consists of executives from ExxonMobil, Chevron, Conoco, Shell Oil, and BP America

2005 Halliburton $1.4 billion billed to US taxpayers unaccounted for

2006 Halliburton surpasses $20 billion in Iraq contracts

Condoleezza Rice, Secretary of State and National Security Advisor: 1991-2000 - Manager of Chevron Oil, International Oil Tanker named after her

Samuel Bodman, Secretary of Energy: government contract given to Lee Raymond (the former CEO of ExxonMobil) in order to develop new policy solutions to the US Energy Crisis

Donald Evans, Former Secretary of Commerce: former CEO and chair of Tom Brown, Inc. (a multi-billion dollar oil company)

Steven Griles, Former Secretary of Interior: former executive and lobbyist for Sunoco oil company

Gale Norton, Former Secretary of Interior: former national chairwoman of the Coalition of Republican Environmental Advocates-funded by BP Amoco, former lobbyist for Delta Petroleum - an oil interest group

Thomas White, Former Secretary of the Army: former Vice Chairman of Enron and a large shareholder of company's stock

AND THE DECEIT OF OIL CONTINUES

And the Bush administration made an ill advised attempt to force a new Iraq Oil and Gas Law on February 15, 2007 which was leaked onto the internet and thus states:

Article 5: Management of Petroleum Resources

The **Federal Oil and Gas Council** shall include: "the Chief Executives of important related petroleum companies" which includes the **CEOs of Exxonmobil, Shell, and Chevron Texaco**

"The **Federal Oil and Gas Council** sets the special instructions for negotiations pertaining to **granting rights or signing Development and Production contracts**, and setting qualification criteria for companies."

Article 13: Exploration and Production Contracts

"On the basis of a Field Development Plan prepared and approved in accordance with this Law and the relevant contract, INOC and other holders of an Exploration and Production right may retain the exclusive right to develop and produce Petroleum within the limits of a Development and Production Area for a period to be determined by the **Federal Oil and Gas Council** varying from fifteen (15) to twenty (20) years, not exceeding twenty (20) years dating from the date of approval of the Field Development Plan, depending on considerations related to optimal oil recovery and utilization of existing infrastructure. In cases which for technical and economic considerations warrant longer Production period, the **Federal Oil and Gas Council**, on newly negotiated terms, has the authority to grant an extension not exceeding five (5) years."

"The appointment of an Operator shall be approved by the Designated Authority, and the procedures for such appointment are stated in the initial Contract, and according to the guidelines issued by the **Federal Oil and Gas Council**, and the Operator should be named in the initial Contract."

Article 40: Existing Contracts

"The **Designated Authority** in the Kurdistan Region will take responsibility to review all existing Exploration and Production contracts with any entity before this law enters into force to ensure harmony with the objectives and general provisions of this law to obtain maximum economic returns to the people of Iraq, taking into consideration the prevailing circumstances at the time at which those contracts were agreed, and in a period not exceeding three (3) months from the date of entry into force of this law. The **Panel of Independent Advisors** will take responsibility to assess the contracts referred to in this Article, and their opinion shall be binding in relation to these contracts." But the **"Designated Authority"** and **"Panel of Independent Advisors"** are not disclosed.

So, we will let the Bush administration and Big Oil claim the oil and do as the Lord commands ... "save the OIL and the WINE", the fornication of oil and the blood of mankind, for as He promised "Truly I say to you, you will not come out of there until you have paid up the last cent." (Matthew 5:26)

LORD MAY THEIR OIL BURN IN THE FIRE

XXI

The Bread the Word of God (NASB)
To Andrew the Prophet Completed
October 18, 2007

God gives us bread to live physically and spiritually

"By the sweat of your face You will eat **bread**, Till you return to the ground, Because from it you were taken; For you are dust, And to dust you shall return." Genesis 3:19

"Then the LORD said to Moses, 'Behold, I will rain **bread** from heaven for you; and the people shall go out and gather a day's portion every day, that I may test them, whether or not they will walk in My instruction.'" Exodus 16:4

"Now this day will be a memorial to you, and you shall celebrate it as a feast to the LORD; throughout your generations you are to celebrate it as a permanent ordinance. Seven days you shall eat unleavened **bread**, but on the first day you shall remove leaven from your houses; for whoever eats anything leavened from the first day until the seventh day, that person shall be cut off from Israel." Exodus 12:14-15

"You shall set the **bread** of the Presence on the table before Me at all times." Exodus 25:30

"He humbled you and let you be hungry, and fed you with manna which you did not know, nor did your fathers know, that He might make you understand that man does not live by **bread** alone, but man lives by everything that proceeds out of the mouth of the LORD." Deuteronomy 8:3

"He gives his **bread** to the hungry and covers the naked with clothing, he keeps his hand from the poor, does not take interest or increase, but executes My ordinances, and walks in My statutes; he will not die for his father's iniquity, he will surely live." Ezekiel 18:16

Mankind chose the bread of wickedness

"For they cannot sleep unless they do evil; And they are robbed of sleep unless they make someone stumble. For they eat the **bread** of wickedness And drink the wine of violence." Proverbs 4:16-17

"Esau said, 'Behold, I am about to die; so of what use then is the birthright to me?' And Jacob said, 'First swear to me'; so he swore to him, and sold his birthright to Jacob. Then Jacob gave Esau **bread** and lentil stew; and he ate and drank, and rose and went on his way. Thus Esau despised his birthright."Genesis 25:32-33

"For I have eaten ashes like **bread** And mingled my drink with weeping. Because of Your indignation and Your wrath, For You have lifted me up and cast me away." Psalms 102:9-10

The Father is the Source of the Word

"Pray, then, in this way: 'Our Father who is in heaven, Hallowed be Your name. Your kingdom come. Your will be done, On earth as it is in heaven. Give us this day our daily **bread**.'" Matthew 6:9-12

"If anyone loves Me, he will keep My **word**; and My Father will love him, and We will come to him and make Our abode with him. He who does not love Me does not keep My **word**s; and the **word** which you hear is not Mine, but the Father's who sent Me." John 14:23-24

Christ came as a man to be the Word of God

"In the beginning was the **Word**, and the **Word** was with God, and the **Word** was God. He was in the beginning with God. All things came into being through Him, and apart from Him nothing came into being that has come into being... And the **Word** became flesh, and dwelt among us, and we saw His glory, glory as of the only begotten from the Father, full of grace and truth." John 1:1-14

'Jesus then said to them, 'Truly, truly, I say to you, it is not Moses who has given you the **bread** out of heaven, but it is My Father who gives you the true **bread** out of heaven. For the **bread** of God is that which comes down out of heaven, and gives life to the world.' Then they said to Him, 'Lord, always give us this **bread**'. Jesus said to them, 'I am the **bread** of life; he who comes to Me will not hunger, and he who believes in Me will never thirst.'" John 6:32-35

"While they were eating, Jesus took some **bread**, and after a blessing, He broke it and gave it to the disciples, and said, 'Take, eat; this is My body.'" Matthew 26:26

Through Christ we become one Bread, one body with Christ

"Is not the cup of blessing which we bless a sharing in the blood of Christ? Is not the **bread** which we break a sharing in the body of Christ? Since there is one **bread**, we who are many are one body; for we all partake of the one **bread**." 1 Corinthians 10:16-17

The Spirit spreads the Word

"And Jesus said to them, 'Watch out and beware of the leaven of the Pharisees and Sadducees.' They began to discuss this among themselves, saying, 'He said that because we did not bring any **bread**.' But Jesus, aware of this, said, 'You men of little faith, why do you discuss among yourselves that you have no **bread**? Do you not yet understand or remember the five loaves of the five thousand, and how many baskets full you picked up? Or the seven loaves of the four thousand, and how many large baskets full you picked up? How is it that you do not understand that I did not speak to you concerning **bread**? But beware of the leaven of the Pharisees and Sadducees.'" Matthew 16:6-11

"Now we have received, not the spirit of the world, but the Spirit who is from God, so that we may know the things freely given to us by God, which things we also speak, not in **word**s taught by human wisdom, but in those taught by the Spirit, combining spiritual thoughts with spiritual **word**s." 1 Corinthians 2:12-13

"But prove yourselves doers of the **word**, and not merely hearers who delude themselves. For if anyone is a hearer of the **word** and not a doer, he is like a man who looks at his natural face in a mirror; for once he has looked at himself and gone away, he has immediately forgotten what kind of person he was." James 1:22-23

"The sower sows the **word**...And those are the ones on whom seed was sown on the good soil; and they hear the **word** and accept it and bear fruit, thirty, sixty, and a hundredfold." Mark 4:14-20

And the WORD will return

"Truly I say to you, this generation will not pass away until all these things take place. Heaven and earth will pass away, but My **word**s will not pass away." Matthew 24:34-35

"He spoke another parable to them, "The kingdom of heaven is like leaven, which a woman took and hid in three pecks of flour until it was all leavened."Matthew 13:33

"And I saw heaven opened, and behold, a white horse, and He who sat on it is called Faithful and True, and in righteousness He judges and wages war. His eyes are a flame of fire, and on His head are many diadems; and He has a name written on Him which no one knows except Himself.. He is clothed with a robe dipped in blood, and His name is called The **Word** of God." Revelation 19:11-13

"Then he said to me, "Write, 'Blessed are those who are invited to the marriage supper of the Lamb.' And he said to me, 'These are true **word**s of God.'" Revelation 19:9

"And He who sits on the throne said, 'Behold, I am making all things new.' And He said, 'Write, for these **word**s are faithful and true.' Then He said to me, 'It is done. I am the Alpha and the Omega, the beginning and the end. I will give to the one who thirsts from the spring of the water of life without cost. He who overcomes will inherit these things, and I will be his God and he will be My son.'" Revelation 21:5-7

The Bread of God is the Word of God

Bread is that which gives sustenance to life. And when God created Adam and Eve, He gave them bread to sustain their bodies, until they returned to dust of the earth, for what comes from the dust must return to the dust. (Genesis 3:19) And when His people complained, that they had no food to sustain them, God in His mercy rained manna, the bread from the heavens. (Exodus 16:4) And He commanded His people to eat, the *unleavened bread* as a memorial, that He had saved them from Egypt. (Exodus 12:14-15) And He commanded His people to leave the bread, at the table of showbread as a memorial, of His presence amongst them in the temple. (Exodus 25:30) And Moses reminded His people, that the bread of this earth is perishable, and man must not live on bread alone, but on the Bread or Word of God. (Deuteronomy 8:3) And the prophets promised that those, who lived on His Bread, and executed His ordinances, and walked in His statutes, would surely live. (Ezekiel 18:16)

But did His people live on the Bread of God, and execute His ordinances, and walk in His statutes? No, for they forsook the Bread of God, and ate the bread of wickedness, and drank of the wine of violence. (Proverbs 4:16-17) And Esau the father of Islam, would forsake his inheritance from his father, for the bread of deceit from Jacob. (Genesis 25:32-33) And the curse of their deception would endure, from that curse until the end of mankind. For by the fruits of man's wickedness, mankind will be destroyed, and will eat the bread of ashes, and drink the cup of weeping. (Psalms 102:9-10)

What is bread? Bread is the food from the earth, which gives us earthly life. And what is the Bread of Life? The Bread of Life is the Word of God, which gives us eternal life. And bread consists of three ingredients: water, grain, and yeast. And water is the sustenance of life on earth, as the Father is the sustenance of life in heaven. And grain is the seed of the bread, as Christ is the Seed of the Word. (Galatians 3:16) And yeast produces carbon dioxide, which causes the bread to rise. And the Spirit produces the fruits of God, which causes His Word to rise. Thus the Bread or Word of God, consists of three ingredients: the Father, the Son, and the Holy Spirit.

Bread consists of water, as the Word of God comes from the Father. For the Lord instructed us to pray, to our Father in heaven this way, "Give us our daily bread." (Matthew 6:9-12) And the Lord taught us the Word of God, which comes the Father who sent Him. For as we know THE SON IS THE WORD, and He was sent from the Father, for "the Word became flesh, and dwelt among us." (John 1:14) And He promised if we followed His Word, that the Father would love us as well. (John 14:23-24)

And God sent His Son to earth as a man, so that He could give us the Word of God. For from the beginning, the Son was the Word of God, who came to dwell amongst us, and was full of truth and grace. (John 1:1-14) For the Father would give us the bread of heaven, for Christ was the manna the Bread from heaven. For as Christ said, "**I am the bread of life**; he who comes to Me will not hunger, and he who believes in Me will never thirst." (John 6:32-35) And in remembrance of His death for mankind, no longer do we leave the bread at the table, for He broke the bread at the table, and gave it to His disciples and said, "Take, eat; this is My body." (Matthew 26:26)

For when we partake of the bread of Christ, we become one bread and one body with Christ.(1 Corinthians 10:16-17) And what is the difference between the bread of Israel and the bread of Christ? The bread of Israel was unleavened, but the bread of Christ is leavened. For it is leavened with the power of the Holy Spirit. (Exodus 12:14-15). And it is the power of the Spirit which causes His Word to rise.

And what is leavening? Leavening is the process of adding yeast, into the bread so that it grows through the process of fermentation. And fermentation is the process, by which yeast digests the sugars in the bread, to produce carbon dioxide in the bread. The carbon dioxide expands in the bread, and causes the bread to rise. And the yeast during the time of Christ, was grown by soaking the bread in wine. What is the leavening of the Bread of God? It is the process by which the Holy Spirit, enters into our lives so that the Bread of Christ, can grow through the Holy Spirit. And the growth of the Holy Spirit, is the process by which our fruits produce works, through the power of the Holy Spirit. And the works of the Holy Spirit rise throughout the nations and cause His Church grow. And the Holy Spirit was given to us, by soaking the Bread in the Wine: by sacrificing His body in His blood.

When Christ fed the crowd with the bread, from five loaves to fill five thousand, it was a foretelling that the kingdom of God would grow to become the leavened bread. For from the feeding from five to five thousand, the Spirit would leaven His kingdom. But He warned not to use the Pharisees' leaven, for their leaven was dead to the Spirit. (Matthew 16:6-11) And what does it mean to leaven His kingdom? It means that the Spirit gives us the Word, and that the Word of God becomes ours. (1 Corinthians 2:12-13) And when the Word of God is ours, then we are made into doers of the Word, for then we can spread the Word of God. (James 1:22-23) And when we become doers of the Word, we multiply the fruits of the Spirit, some "thirty, sixty, and a hundredfold." (Mark 4:14-20)

And the Lord promised that all would see His return, "Truly I say to you, this generation will not pass away until all these things take place. Heaven and earth will pass away, but My words will not pass away." (Matthew 24:34-35) And by His good grace, a new leavened kingdom has been prepared for all. For one of one thousand have entered His gate, but what was five is now five thousand. And now all men shall enter His gates. (Matthew 13:33)

And when the last bowl of wrath has been poured, the One who is Faithful and True, will wage war with the ruler of this world. For His name is Bread and **"The Word of God."** (Revelation 19:11-13) And the true Word of God is this, that all men are invited to His supper. (Revelation 19:9) For when the ruler of this world has been vanquished, Christ the Lamb who is Faithful and True, will say these words which are faithful and true, "It is done. I am the Alpha and the Omega, the beginning and the end. I will give to the one who thirsts from the spring of the water of life without cost. He who overcomes will inherit these things, and I will be his God and he will be My son." (Revelation 21:5-7)

XXII

Salt is Faithfulness (NASB)
To Andrew the Prophet
Completed October 22, 2007

"You are the **salt** of the earth; but if the **salt** has become tasteless, how can it be made **salty** again? It is no longer good for anything, except to be thrown out and trampled under foot by men." Matthew 5:13

Salt destroyed Lot's wife for her lack of faith

"Then the LORD rained on Sodom and Gomorrah brimstone and fire from the LORD out of heaven, and He overthrew those cities, and all the valley, and all the inhabitants of the cities, and what grew on the ground. But his wife, from behind him, looked back, and she became a pillar of **salt**." Genesis 19:24-26

Salt and Faith is a preservative and seasoning

"In addition to all, taking up the shield of **faith** with which you will be able to extinguish all the flaming arrows of the evil one." Ephesians 6:16

"So that the proof of your **faith**, being more precious than gold which is perishable, even though tested by fire, may be found to result in praise and glory and honor at the revelation of Jesus Christ." 1 Peter 1:7

"Let your speech always be with grace, as though seasoned with **salt**, so that you will know how you should respond to each person." Colossians 4:6

God made a covenant of salt

"All the offerings of the holy gifts, which the sons of Israel offer to the LORD, I have given to you and your sons and your daughters with you, as a perpetual allotment. It is an everlasting covenant of **salt** before the LORD to you and your descendants with you." Number 18:19

"Then the LORD said to Moses, 'Take for yourself spices, stacte and onycha and galbanum, spices with pure frankincense; there shall be an equal part of each. With it you shall make incense, a perfume, the work of a perfumer, **salted**, pure, and holy. You shall beat some of it very fine, and put part of it before the testimony in the tent of meeting where I will meet with you; it shall be most holy to you. The incense which you shall make, you shall not make in the same proportions for yourselves; it shall be holy to you for the LORD.'" Exodus 30:34-37

"Every grain offering of yours, moreover, you shall season with **salt**, so that the **salt** of the covenant of your God shall not be lacking from your grain offering; with all your offerings you shall offer **salt**." Leviticus 2:13

Salt can destroy

"'All its land is brimstone and **salt**, a burning waste, unsown and unproductive, and no grass grows in it, like the overthrow of Sodom and Gomorrah, Admah and Zeboiim, which the LORD overthrew in His anger and in His wrath.' All the nations will say, 'Why has the LORD done thus to this land? Why this great outburst of anger?' Then men will say, 'Because they forsook the covenant of the LORD, the God of their fathers, which He made with them when He brought them out of the land of Egypt.'"Deuteronomy 29:23-25

"He changes rivers into a wilderness And springs of water into a thirsty ground; A fruitful land into a **salt** waste, Because of the wickedness of those who dwell in it." Psalms 107:33-34

Salt is Faith

"You are the **salt** of the earth; but if the **salt** has become tasteless, how can it be made salty again? It is no longer good for anything, except to be thrown out and trampled under foot by men." Matthew 5:13

"For everyone will be **salted** with fire. **Salt** is good; but if the **salt** becomes **unsalty**, with what will you make it **salty** again? Have **salt** in yourselves, and be at peace with one another." Mark 9:49

Faith is Believing without seeing

"But the centurion said, 'Lord, I am not worthy for You to come under my roof, but just say the word, and my servant will be healed. For I also am a man under authority, with soldiers under me; and I say to this one, 'Go!' and he goes, and to another, 'Come!' and he comes, and to my slave, 'Do this!' and he does it.' Now when Jesus heard this, He marveled and said to those who were following, 'Truly I say to you, I have not found such great **faith** with anyone in Israel.'" Matthew 8:8-10

"Therefore, being always of good courage, and knowing that while we are at home in the body we are absent from the Lord-- for we walk by **faith**, not by sight" 2 Corinthians 5:6

"Now **faith** is the assurance of things hoped for, the conviction of things not seen. For by it the men of old gained approval. By faith we understand that the worlds were prepared by the word of God, so that what is seen was not made out of things which are visible." Hebrews 11:1-3

Faith is holding up to persecution

"Be on the alert, stand firm in the **faith**, act like men, be strong. Let all that you do be done in love." 1 Corinthians 16:13-14

"And we desire that each one of you show the same diligence so as to realize the full assurance of hope until the end, so that you will not be sluggish, but imitators of those who through **faith** and patience inherit the promises." Hebrews 6:11-12

"Consider it all joy, my brethren, when you encounter various trials, knowing that the testing of your **faith** produces endurance." James 1:2-3

Christ the King is FAITHFUL

"And I saw heaven opened, and behold, a white horse, and He who sat on it is called **Faithful** and True, and in righteousness He judges and wages war. His eyes are a flame of fire, and on His head are many diadems; and He has a name written on Him which no one knows except Himself. He is clothed with a robe dipped in blood, and His name is called The Word of God." Revelation 19:11-13

Salt is Faith

"Then the LORD rained on Sodom and Gomorrah brimstone and fire from the LORD out of heaven, and He overthrew those cities, and all the valley, and all the inhabitants of the cities, and what grew on the ground. But his wife, from behind him, looked back, and she became a pillar of **salt**."(Genesis 19:24-26) Salt has two natures it preserves and destroys. Salt preserves man and the Word through faith. But as Lot's wife proved by her lack of faith, our faith can be trampled and destroyed.

In the days of our forefathers, salt was a commodity more valuable than gold. And as a follower of God, faith is a commodity more valuable than gold. (1 Peter 1:7) Salt serves two purposes, it functions as a preservative and as a seasoning. And salt acts as a preservative by protecting our food, from microorganisms which are destroyed by the salt. And faith preserves bread which is Word of God, by shielding us from the "arrows of the evil one." (Ephesians 6:16) And salt acts as seasoning by enhancing the flavor of food. And faith seasons our speech of God, and enhances the Word of God. (Colossians 4:6)

When God made a covenant with His people, He made them a covenant of salt. (Number 18:19) For by giving them the salt of the earth, He gave them His faithful promise, that His people would inherit the promised land, if they would keep His covenant. "Now then, if you will indeed obey My voice and keep My covenant, then you shall be My own possession among all the peoples, for all the earth is Mine; and you shall be to Me a kingdom of priests and a holy nation." (Exodus 19:5-6) And by His covenant of faithfulness, He promised His people that He would return, and He and His people would rule all the nations. "Behold, a king will reign righteously And princes will rule justly." (Isaiah 32:1)

And for His faithful covenant, God commanded His people to salt the perfume, at the tent of the meeting place. (Exodus 30:34-37) And He commanded them to salt their grain offerings. (Leviticus 2:13) But His covenant of salt was not salt of the earth, but the salt of faithfulness to obey His commands. But His people refused the salt of the covenant, and trampled the salt of His faithfulness. And for their lack of faith, and for not keeping His covenant, God destroyed their land with the salt. (Deuteronomy 29:23-25) Thus He turned "a fruitful land into a salt waste, because of the wickedness of those who dwell in it." (Psalms 107:33-34) For salted fields become wastelands, because the crops die when they are salted. For when the arid deserts were irrigated, the watering would cause the salt in the soil to rise. And when Israel was conquered by the nations, their fields were salted to render them useless. And thus their fields became salted, and thus their fruit became barren.

But by God's kindness and forgiveness, He sent His Son to bring us His salt, the salt of steadfastness and the gift of faith. And what is salt? Salt is sodium chloride, a crystalline and colorless solid. And how is salt formed? It is formed by replacing the hydrogen ion of an acid with a metallic ion. Thus, the balance of the chemical equation is as follows:

$$NaCl + H2O \leftrightarrow Hcl + NaOH$$

or

$$Salt + Water \leftrightarrow Acid + Base$$

And as we know, acids and bases are toxic wastes that must be thrown out. And as Christ said "You are the salt of the earth; but if the salt has become tasteless, how can it be made salty again? It is no longer good for anything, except to be thrown out and trampled under foot by men." (Matthew 5:13) But following the path of Christ is difficult, for as He promised, all must face the fire of persecution. (Mark 9:49) For as we know, God is water and we are "the salt of the earth", and if acids and bases are thrown out, then the equation becomes:

Persecution and Faith

Followers of Christ + God ⟨ Persecution and Faith ⟩ **Thrown out**

For though you may be a follower of God, you still may not be among His elect, for if you cannot live by faith, or stand firm through the persecutions of men, then you will become salt that is tasteless, and thrown out and trampled under foot by men. And the answer to the question "how can it be made salty again?" is through **FAITH**. For God wants His children to follow Christ, and by faith to stand firm to the persecutions of men, and by faith remain salt of the earth.

And what is faith? Faith is believing without seeing. Remember the centurion who asked the Lord, "only say the word and my servant will be healed." And our Lord replied "Truly I say to you, I have not found such great faith with anyone in Israel." (Matthew 8:8-10) So too must we learn to "walk by faith, and not by sight". (2 Corinthians 5:6) For we look forward to the hope of what will come, for the generations have had faith in what was not seen, in the faithfulness of what God has promised will be. (Hebrews 11:1-3)

And by faith, we are called on to be strong, upholding His Words that sustain us, and bestowing the love He exemplified. (1 Corinthians 16:13) And we are commanded to be diligent, in spreading the Truth and His Word. (Hebrews 6:11-12) And we are called on to endure all the trials. For through the fires of persecution, we develop the endurance, to hope in the faithful promises that will come. (James 1:2-3)

The time is near! For the faithful generations who have remained salt , who have lived by faith, who have endured the persecutions, who have stood firmly on His Word; the One who is Faithful and True shall return. Yes He is the Lamb and the Word of God. For He is our Lord the faithful King. (Revelation 19:11-13)

XXIII

Christ is the Good Shepherd (NASB)
To Andrew the Prophet Completed
October 23, 2010

" I am the good **shepherd**, and I know My own and My own know Me, even as the Father knows Me and I know the Father; and I lay down My life for the **sheep**." John 10:11

The only unblemished lamb is Christ

"Isaac spoke to Abraham his father and said, 'My father!' And he said, 'Here I am, my son.' And he said, 'Behold, the fire and the wood, but where is the **lamb** for the burnt offering?' Abraham said, 'God will provide for Himself the **lamb** for the burnt offering, my son.' So the two of them walked on together." Genesis 22:7-8

"Your **lamb** shall be an unblemished male a year old; you may take it from the sheep or from the goats. You shall keep it until the fourteenth day of the same month, then the whole assembly of the congregation of Israel is to kill it at twilight." Exodus 12:5-6

"'What are your multiplied sacrifices to Me?' Says the LORD. 'I have had enough of burnt offerings of rams And the fat of fed cattle; And I take no pleasure in the blood of bulls, **lambs** or goats. When you come to appear before Me, Who requires of you this trampling of My courts? Bring your worthless offerings no longer, Incense is an abomination to Me. New moon and sabbath, the calling of assemblies-- I cannot endure iniquity and the solemn assembly. I hate your new moon festivals and your appointed feasts, They have become a burden to Me; I am weary of bearing them. So when you spread out your hands in prayer, I will hide My eyes from you; Yes, even though you multiply prayers, I will not listen. Your hands are covered with blood. Wash yourselves, make yourselves clean; Remove the evil of your deeds from My sight. Cease to do evil, Learn to do good; Seek justice, Reprove the ruthless, Defend the orphan, Plead for the widow.'" Isaiah 1:11-17

"All of us like sheep have gone astray, Each of us has turned to his own way; But the LORD has caused the iniquity of us all To fall on Him. He was oppressed and He was afflicted, Yet He did not open His mouth; Like a **lamb** that is led to slaughter, And like a sheep that is silent before its shearers, So He did not open His mouth... Therefore, I will allot Him a portion with the great, And He will divide the booty with the strong; Because He poured out Himself to death, And was numbered with the transgressors; Yet He Himself bore the sin of many, And interceded for the transgressors." Isaiah 53:6-12

"If you address as Father the One who impartially judges according to each one's work, conduct yourselves in fear during the time of your stay on earth; knowing that you were not redeemed with perishable things like silver or gold from your futile way of life inherited from your forefathers, but with precious blood, as of a **lamb** unblemished and spotless, the blood of Christ" 1 Peter 1:17-18

Christ the Lamb is the Shepherd

"Oh, give ear, **Shepherd** of Israel, You who lead Joseph like a flock; You who are enthroned above the cherubim, shine forth!" Psalms 80:1

"The words of wise men are like goads, and masters of these collections are like well-driven nails; they are given by one **Shepherd**." Ecclesiastes 12:11

"I am the good **shepherd**; the good **shepherd** lays down His life for the sheep. He who is a hired hand, and not a **shepherd**, who is not the owner of the sheep, sees the wolf coming, and leaves the sheep and flees, and the wolf snatches them and scatters them. He flees because he is a hired hand and is not concerned about the sheep. I am the good **shepherd**, and I know My own and My own know Me, even as the Father knows Me and I know the Father; and I lay down My life for the sheep." John 10:11-15

He sends us out as lambs

"And He was saying to them, 'The harvest is plentiful, but the laborers are few; therefore beseech the Lord of the harvest to send out laborers into His harvest. Go; behold, I send you out as **lambs** in the midst of wolves.'" Luke 10:2-3

" I said to him, 'My lord, you know.' And he said to me, 'These are the ones who come out of the great tribulation, and they have washed their robes and made them white in the blood of the **Lamb**. For this reason, they are before the throne of God; and they serve Him day and night in His temple; and He who sits on the throne will spread His tabernacle over them.'" Revelation 7:14-15

"'Let us rejoice and be glad and give the glory to Him, for the marriage of the **Lamb** has come and His bride has made herself ready.' It was given to her to clothe herself in fine linen, bright and clean; for the fine linen is the righteous acts of the saints" Revelation 19:7-8

"And when the Chief **Shepherd** appears, you will receive the unfading crown of glory." 1 Peter 5:4

The shepherds of this age have sinned greatly

"Many **shepherds** have ruined My vineyard, They have trampled down My field; They have made My pleasant field A desolate wilderness. It has been made a desolation, Desolate, it mourns before Me; The whole land has been made desolate, Because no man lays it to heart." Jeremiah 12:10-11

"For thus says the LORD to me, 'As the lion or the young lion growls over his prey, Against which a band of **shepherds** is called out, And he will not be terrified at their voice nor disturbed at their noise, So will the LORD of hosts come down to wage war on Mount Zion and on its hill.'" Isaiah 31:4

"'Woe to the **shepherds** who are destroying and scattering the sheep of My pasture!' declares the LORD. Therefore thus says the LORD God of Israel concerning the **shepherds** who are tending My people: 'You have scattered My flock and driven them away, and have not attended to them; behold, I am about to attend to you for the evil of your deeds,' declares the LORD. 'Then I Myself will gather the remnant of My flock out of all the countries where I have driven them and bring them back to their pasture, and they will be fruitful and multiply. I will also raise up **shepherds** over them and they will tend them; and they will not be afraid any longer, nor be terrified, nor will any be missing,' declares the LORD." Jeremiah 23:1-4

And the Great Shepherd will return

"But when the Son of Man comes in His glory, and all the angels with Him, then He will sit on His glorious throne. All the nations will be gathered before Him; and He will separate them from one another, as the **shepherd** separates the sheep from the goats; and He will put the sheep on His right, and the goats on the left. Then the King will say to those on His right, 'Come, you who are blessed of My Father, inherit the kingdom prepared for you from the foundation of the world.'" Matthew 25:31-34

"Worthy is the **Lamb** that was slain to receive power and riches and wisdom and might and honor and glory and blessing. And every created thing which is in heaven and on the earth and under the earth and on the sea, and all things in them, I heard saying, 'To Him who sits on the throne, and to the **Lamb**, be blessing and honor and glory and dominion forever and ever.' And the four living creatures kept saying, 'Amen.' And the elders fell down and worshiped." Revelation 5:12-14

"I have other sheep, which are not of this fold; I must bring them also, and they will hear My voice; and they will become one flock with one **shepherd**. For this reason the Father loves Me, because I lay down My life so that I may take it again." John 10:16-17

"I saw no temple in it, for the Lord God the Almighty and the **Lamb** are its temple. And the city has no need of the sun or of the moon to shine on it, for the glory of God has illumined it, and its lamp is the **Lamb**." Revelation 21:22-23

We Will be Lambs

God is a merciful God, for He sent His Son to be the Lamb, for His sheep the flock of the earth. When Abraham was told to sacrifice Isaac, the Lord withheld His hand from his son. (Genesis 22:7-8) And He spared the lives of His chosen people, when He passed them over from Egypt. For He commanded them to sacrifice a lamb, and to spread its blood "on the two doorposts, and on the lintel of the houses in which they eat it", so the angel of death would pass over them. (Exodus 12:5-6) And on the fourteenth day of the month, the lamb of the Passover was sacrificed. And on the fourteenth day of the month, the Lamb of Christ was sacrificed. And on the fourteenth day of the month, the lamb that is His witness will be sacrificed.

But did God truly want the sacrifice of the lambs? NO. For what He wanted was the sacrifice of obedience, that His people would obey His commandments. For He commanded a different sacrifice, "Wash yourselves, make yourselves clean; Remove the evil of your deeds from My sight. Cease to do evil, Learn to do good; Seek justice, Reprove the ruthless, Defend the orphan, Plead for the widow." (Isaiah 1:11-17) But His people sinned greatly and transgressed His commandments, and would sacrifice the lamb to be reconciled with God. And by their transgressions and sins, He removed His blessings from His people. And the punishment and suffering was great, for all of His sheep had gone astray.

But God in His infinite mercy, promised He would come as the Lamb, and by the blood of His sacrifice, His people would be saved. For He was Lamb that would cover their transgressions. (Isaiah 53:6-12) And when His people passed over from Egypt, God asked for the sacrifice of an "unblemished lamb". But truly there is only one unblemished lamb, that is sacrificed for the sins of the world; for *He is the Lamb of God who takes away the sins of the world*. (1 Peter 1:17-18)

And what is a lamb? A lamb is a sheep that is yoked by a shepherd. Yet the Shepherd became a Lamb, so that mankind could be free. For before He was the Lamb, He was the Shepherd of His people. He was the Shepherd who guided His people, out of the famine and into Egypt. (Psalms 80:1) And when His flock returned to their land, He shepherded the kings who ruled over His kingdom. (Ecclesiastes 12:11) And as the Father knows His Son, so does the Son know His sheep. For He is the true Shepherd who lays down His life, so that His sheep may inherit eternal life. (John 10:10-15)

For the Lamb was sacrificed on the cross, but on the third day the Lamb rose again. For He came as the Lamb to die for mankind, and returned as the Shepherd to gather His sheep. For not only did He die for our sins, but He died to show us the true sacrifice of love. And He commanded His flock to follow His footsteps, for they too were "lambs in the midst of wolves." (Luke 10:2-3) And the price they paid was great indeed, for in the image of Christ they became sacrificial lambs. But for their sacrifice their rewards will be great. For on that glorious Day, they will rise in the clouds, having washed their robes white, with the blood of the Lamb. (Revelation 7:14-15) For they are the bride of the Groom, and will wear the fine linen of their righteousness. (Revelation 19:7-8) And they will receive the crown of glory, (1 Peter 5:4) and will fear no more, and will be His shepherds, and will tend to His sheep. (Jeremiah 23:4)

But what of the shepherds of this age? For the prophets had foretold, that the shepherds of this age would leave our lands desolate, for they have refused to lay His statutes to heart. (Jeremiah 12:10-11) And despite all the warnings, our rulers have been told, of the folly of their ways, they refuse to heed His warnings. (Isaiah 31:4) But woe to these shepherds, to al-Sadr to Bush to Cheney and Ahmadinejad, for they have destroyed and scattered the sheep. Behold, God will soon tend to you for the evil of your ways! (Jeremiah 23:1-3)

Yes the time is near "when the Son of Man comes in His glory, and all the angels with Him, then He will sit on His glorious throne." And He will separate His sheep, on the right for His glory, and on the left for the slaughter. (Matthew 25:31-34) And when they have gathered on that glorious day, His remnant will bow at the throne of the Lamb. And they will sing "Worthy is the Lamb that was slain to receive power and riches and wisdom and might and honor and glory and blessing. And every created thing which is in heaven and on the earth and under the earth and on the sea, and all things in them, to Him who sits on the throne, and to the Lamb, be blessing and honor and glory and dominion forever and ever. Amen" (Revelation 5:12-14)

And the bowls of wrath will be poured, and the judgment will be great indeed. But by God's goodness and grace, all things shall be forgiven, for He is a forgiving God. And once the penalty has been paid, all men will return to the Father. For as He said, "I have other sheep, which are not of this fold; I must bring them also, and they will hear My voice; and they will become one flock with one shepherd. For this reason the Father loves Me, because I lay down My life so that I may take it again." (John 10:16-17) For Christ is the unblemished Lamb, for He came and died for mankind. And once the ruler of this world has been slain, all will be brought by the Lamb into His city, and it will have "no need of the sun or of the moon to shine on it, for the glory of God has illumined it, and its lamp is the Lamb." (Revelation 21:22-23)

XXIV

He Returns with Vengeance as the Lion (NASB)
To Andrew the Prophet
Completed October 27, 2007

The Father controls all things, including the lions

"The terror of a king is like the growling of a **lion**; He who provokes him to anger forfeits his own life." Proverbs 20:2

"Then he said to him, 'Because you have not listened to the voice of the LORD, behold, as soon as you have departed from me, a **lion** will kill you.' And as soon as he had departed from him a **lion** found him and killed him." 1 Kings 20:36

"At the beginning of their living there, they did not fear the LORD; therefore the LORD sent **lions** among them which killed some of them." 2 Kings 17:25

"The king's wrath is like the roaring of a **lion**, But his favor is like dew on the grass." Proverbs 19:12

"My God sent His angel and shut the **lions'** mouths and they have not harmed me, inasmuch as I was found innocent before Him; and also toward you, O king, I have committed no crime." Daniel 6:22

The Lion's return is foretold

"Its roaring is like a **lioness**, and it roars like young **lions**; It growls as it seizes the prey And carries it off with no one to deliver it. And it will growl over it in that day like the roaring of the sea. If one looks to the land, behold, there is darkness and distress; Even the light is darkened by its clouds." Isaiah 5:29-30

"For thus says the LORD to me, 'As the **lion** or the young **lion** growls over his prey, Against which a band of shepherds is called out, And he will not be terrified at their voice nor disturbed at their noise, So will the LORD of hosts come down to wage war on Mount Zion and on its hill...For in that day every man will cast away his silver idols and his gold idols, which your sinful hands have made for you as a sin. And the Assyrian will fall by a sword not of man, And a sword not of man will devour him.'" Isaiah 31:4-8

The beasts are George Bush Jr., Richard Cheney, Donald Rumsfeld and Moqtada al-Sadr

"Daniel said, 'I was looking in my vision by night, and behold, the four winds of heaven were stirring up the great sea. And four great beasts were coming up from the sea, different from one another. The first was like a **lion** and had the wings of an eagle. I kept looking until its wings were plucked, and it was lifted up from the ground and made to stand on two feet like a man; a human mind also was given to it. And behold, another beast, a second one, resembling a bear. And it was raised up on one side, and three ribs were in its mouth between its teeth; and thus they said to it, 'Arise, devour much meat! After this I kept looking, and behold, another one, like a leopard, which had on its back four wings of a bird; the beast also had four heads, and dominion was given to it. After this I kept looking in the night visions, and behold, a fourth beast, dreadful and terrifying and extremely strong; and it had large iron teeth. It devoured and crushed and trampled down the remainder with its feet; and it was different from all the beasts that were before it, and it had ten horns. While I was contemplating the horns, behold, another horn, a little one, came up among them, and three of the first horns were pulled out by the roots before it; and behold, this horn possessed eyes like the eyes of a man and a mouth uttering great boasts.'" Daniel 7:2-8

"And the dragon stood on the sand of the seashore. Then I saw a beast coming up out of the sea, having ten horns and seven heads, and on his horns were ten diadems, and on his heads were blasphemous names. And the beast which I saw was like a leopard, and his feet were like those of a bear, and his mouth like the mouth of a **lion**. And the dragon gave him his power and his throne and great authority." Revelation 13:1-2

His 144,000 is the creature with four heads

"As for the form of their faces, each had the face of a man; all four had the face of a **lion** on the right and the face of a bull on the left, and all four had the face of an eagle." Ezekiel 1:10

"The first creature was like a **lion**, and the second creature like a calf, and the third creature had a face like that of a man, and the fourth creature was like a flying eagle. And the four living creatures, each one of them having six wings, are full of eyes around and within; and day and night they do not cease to say, 'HOLY, HOLY, HOLY is THE LORD GOD, THE ALMIGHTY, WHO WAS AND WHO IS AND WHO IS TO COME.'" Revelation 4:7-8

"the twenty-four elders fall down before Him who sits on the throne and worship Him who lives forever and ever, and cast their crowns before the throne" Revelation 4:10

The 144,000 have the favor of the King

"The wicked flee when no one is pursuing, But the righteous are bold as a **lion**." Proverbs 28:1

"Judah, your brothers shall praise you; Your hand shall be on the neck of your enemies; Your father's sons shall bow down to you. Judah is a **lion's** whelp; From the prey, my son, you have gone up. He couches, he lies down as a **lion**, And as a **lion**, who dares rouse him up? The scepter shall not depart from Judah, Nor the ruler's staff from between his feet, Until Shiloh comes, And to him shall be the obedience of the peoples. He ties his foal to the vine, And his donkey's colt to the choice vine; He washes his garments in wine, And his robes in the blood of grapes." Genesis 49:8-11

"There were six steps to the throne and a round top to the throne at its rear, and arms on each side of the seat, and two **lions** standing beside the arms. Twelve **lions** were standing there on the six steps on the one side and on the other; nothing like it was made for any other kingdom." 1 Kings 10:19-20

And in the end, the Lamb will be victorious

"Stop weeping; behold, the **Lion** that is from the tribe of Judah, the Root of David, has overcome so as to open the book and its seven seals." Revelation 5:5

"A highway will be there, a roadway, And it will be called the Highway of Holiness. The unclean will not travel on it, But it will be for him who walks that way, And fools will not wander on it. No **lion** will be there, Nor will any vicious beast go up on it; These will not be found there. But the redeemed will walk there, And the ransomed of the LORD will return And come with joyful shouting to Zion, With everlasting joy upon their heads. They will find gladness and joy, And sorrow and sighing will flee away." Isaiah 35:8-10

The Lion is the Ruler

The lion is called the king of the kingdom, for the lion has great power and strength, the power to destroy and the strength to rule. And those who have served the kings of the earth, they will be subject to the destruction of the Lion. But those who have served the "King of all King's", they shall receive the strength of the Lion.

The Father controls all things, for He controls the destruction of the lion. For "the terror of a king is like the growling of a lion; He who provokes him to anger forfeits his own life." (Proverbs 20:2) For did He not kill, the sons who transgressed Him, with the deadly paws of a lion? (1 Kings 20:36) And did He not kill, those who did not fear Him, by the might of the lions jaws? (2 Kings 17:25) But though "the king's wrath is like the roaring of a lion", "his favor is like dew on the grass." (Proverbs 19:12) And the Lord shut the mouth of the lion, when Daniel was thrown in the pit, for it was by his obedience that he was saved. (Daniel 6:22)

And Daniel foretold that the beasts would come, for the beasts of the ages are here! "And four great beasts were coming up from the sea, different from one another. The first was like a lion and had the wings of an eagle. I kept looking until its wings were plucked, and it was lifted up from the ground and made to stand on two feet like a man; a human mind also was given to it." (Daniel 7:3-4) For the lion with the wings of an eagle is George Bush. For he comes through the sea from America, and the "eagle" makes war with Iraq. And the first wing is our military power, and the second is our economic strength. But because of the boldness and lies of the beast, his wings and his power will be torn, for now he must stand and be judged as a man.

"And behold, another beast, a second one, resembling a bear. And it was raised up on one side, and three ribs were in its mouth between its teeth; and thus they said to it, 'Arise, devour much meat!'" (Daniel 7:5) And the bear that devours three ribs is Richard Cheney. For like a bear he ravages and devours, all the nations for his own selfish gain. And the ribs are three countries he consumes: Kuwait, Afghanistan, and Iraq. For through his corruption and evil deception, he would assist Halliburton in devouring them all.

"After this I kept looking, and behold, another one, like a leopard, which had on its back four wings of a bird; the beast also had four heads, and dominion was given to it." (Daniel 7:6) And the leopard with four heads is Moqtada al-Sadr, who like a leopard has great cunning and stealth. He will unify the four heads or nations, that will fight against the whole world. (Iraq, Iran, Pakistan, and Libya) And the four wings symbolize his authority, through religious and family connections, to bring the four nations together.

"After this I kept looking in the night visions, and behold, a fourth beast, dreadful and terrifying and extremely strong; and it had large iron teeth. It devoured and crushed and trampled down the remainder with its feet; and it was different from all the beasts that were before it, and it had ten horns." (Daniel 7:7) This dreadful and terrifying beast is the coalition, of the ten horns or nations they will fight. And these ten nations will be: the United States, Canada, England, Germany, Australia, New Zealand, South Korea, Russia, China, and Saudi Arabia. And the beast's iron teeth is their strength, and the strength of these ten is immense. For their unified strength is so insurmountable, that the four will not have the strength to fight them ... that is except through nuclear warfare.

"While I was contemplating the horns, behold, another horn, a little one, came up among them, and three of the first horns were pulled out by the roots before it; and behold, this horn possessed eyes like the eyes of a man and a mouth uttering great boasts." (Daniel 7:8) And the little horn is Moqtada al-Sadr, and through the beast's lies and deceptions, he will overtake the other three horns. For from his mouth He utters great boasts, "No, no Satan, No, no USA, No, no occupation, No, no Israel" (AP May 25, 2007)

And the Bible foretold of the beast by sea, for the beast of the sea is George Bush Jr, and his cohorts are Richard Cheney and Donald Rumsfeld. "And he stood on the sand of the seashore. And I saw a beast coming out of the sea, having ten horns and seven heads, and on his horns were ten diadems, and on his heads were blasphemous names." (Revelation 13:1) And the beast from the sea is George Bush and his cohorts. For they come from the US, Babylon the Great, to make war with Iraq , Babylon of old. And the ten horns are the ten lies of Bush (1. Uniting the country, 2. Building the country, 3. Helping the hurricane victims in Louisiana, 4. Capturing Osama Bin Laden, 5. Weapons of mass destruction, 6. "Mission accomplished", 7. Torturing of prisoners, 8. Reducing the budget deficit, 9. Concentrating resources to stop terrorism, 10. Upholding the US Constitution). And the seven heads are seven countries involved in the war, either openly or covertly to save their oil-currency. (US, England, Spain, Saudi Arabia, Japan, Australia, Russia) For their ultimate goal was to control the world's currency, by keeping the currency in petrodollars, and preventing OPEC from converting their oil-currency into Euros. And the ten diadems are the ten sins of Bush. (1. Lies about the reason for attacking Iraq, 2. Incompetence, 3. Ignorance, 4. Errors against terrorism, 5. Isolation from allies, 6. Violations of the Geneva Convention, 7. Violations of domestic laws, 8. False Christianity, 9. Fiscal ineptitude, 10. Murder of more than 1 million Iraqis and more than 4000 US troops).

"And the beast which I saw was like a leopard, and his feet were like those of a bear, and his mouth like the mouth of a lion. And the dragon gave him his power and his throne and great authority." (Revelation 13:2) And the beast is like a leopard, which uses stealth and deception, and his name is Donald Rumsfeld. And the beast has feet like a bear, which tramples on all the nations, and his name is Richard Cheney. And the beast has a mouth like a lion, who boasts prideful and godless words, and his name is George Bush Jr. And Satan gave them great power, but only for a short period, to bring the nations to ruin.

The prophets of old foretold, that the Lion would return in the clouds. And in great vengeance and anger, He will come in the clouds, to darken the days of those who have transgressed Him. (Isaiah 5:29-30) And the Lion and His army will wage a great war, and the nations will fall by the sword. (Isaiah 31:4-8) For as was foretold, "He is clothed with a robe dipped in blood, and His name is called The Word of God. And the armies which are in heaven, clothed in fine linen, white and clean, were following Him on white horses." (Revelation 19:13-14)

And the prophets foretold, that the creature with four heads will worship the Lion, for the creature is the prophets and martyrs and saints, who will rise with our Lord in the clouds. And they will bow down and glorify His name. "As for the form of their faces, each had the face of a man; all four had the face of a lion on the right and the face of a bull on the left, and all four had the face of an eagle." (Ezekiel 1:10) For the creature was made in the likeness of God. And the face of the man is the face of the Father. And the face of the lion is Christ the Lion. And the face of the bull is Christ the Lamb. And the face of the eagle is the Holy Spirit. And the creature will glorify the King, "the first creature was like a lion, and the second creature like a calf, and the third creature had a face like that of a man, and the fourth creature was like a flying eagle. And the four living creatures, each one of them having six wings, are full of eyes around and within; and day and night they do not cease to say, 'Holy, Holy, Holy is the Lord God, The Almighty, who was and is and is to come.'" (Revelation 4:7-8) And the twenty-four wings are the authority of the twenty-four archangels, who have guided them. (Revelation 4:10) And "day and night they do not cease to say Holy, Holy, Holy is the Lord God"; for they worship in the new kingdom where "the city has no need of the sun or the moon to shine upon it, for the glory of God has illumined it, and its lamp is the Lamb." (Revelation 21:23)

When the Lion returns the wicked will flee, but His people will be bold as the lions. (Proverbs 28:1) And Isaac foretold of the tribe of Judah, that the eleven tribes would bow before them, for they are of the Lion's whelp. (Genesis 49:8-10) And the tribe of Judah will be victorious, for they have washed their "garments in wine", and their robes in the "blood of grapes". (Genesis 49:11) For His bride has paid the price, "they have washed their robes and made them white in the blood of the Lamb".(Revelation 7:14) And Solomon built the temple, in the semblance of the kingdom, for besides the throne of the Lion, there were "two lions standing besides the arms". (1 Kings 10:19) For a lion will sit on His right hand, and a lion will sit on His left hand, for as the Lord said "to sit on My right and on My left, this is not Mine to give, but it is for those for whom it has been prepared by My Father." (Matthew 20:23) And on the steps to the throne, there were "twelve lions standing there on the six steps on the one side and on the other" (1 Kings 10:20) For the twelve lions are His twelve apostles who will judge the nations, "truly I say to you, that you who have followed Me, in the regeneration when the Son of Man will sit on His glorious throne, you also shall sit upon twelve thrones, judging the twelve tribes of Israel." (Matthew 19:28)

And the Judgment Day will come soon, for the Lion will return and the Lamb will overcome, so as to open the book and its seals. (Revelation 5:5) But though the wrath will be great, the Lamb will overcome and "a highway will be there, a roadway, and it will be called the Highway of Holiness." And the Lamb will be victorious, and "the ransomed of the LORD will return and come with joyful shouting to Zion, with everlasting joy upon their heads. They will find gladness and joy, and sorrow and sighing will flee away." (Isaiah 35:8-10)

XXV

Peace is Becoming a Child of God (NASB)
To Andrew the Prophet
Completed October 30, 2007

"Blessed are the **peacemakers**, for they shall be called **sons** of God." Matthew 5:9

Christ came as the peace offering

"He sent young men of the **sons** of Israel, and they offered burnt offerings and sacrificed young bulls as **peace** offerings to the LORD." Exodus 24:5

"Even though you offer up to Me burnt offerings and your grain offerings, I will not accept them; And I will not even look at the **peace** offerings of your fatlings." Amos 5:22

"For a child will be born to us, a **son** will be given to us; And the government will rest on His shoulders; And His name will be called Wonderful Counselor, Mighty God, Eternal Father, Prince of **Peace**." Isaiah 9:6

"And suddenly there appeared with the angel a multitude of the heavenly host praising God and saying, Glory to God in the highest, And on earth **peace** among men with whom He is pleased." Luke 2:13

To be at peace we must have faith in God

"Therefore, having been justified by faith, we have **peace** with God through our Lord Jesus Christ" Romans 5:1

"For everyone will be salted with fire. Salt is good; but if the salt becomes unsalty, with what will you make it salty again? Have salt in yourselves, and be at **peace** with one another." Mark 9:49-50

"But the woman fearing and trembling, aware of what had happened to her, came and fell down before Him and told Him the whole truth. And He said to her, "**Daughter**, your **faith** has made you well; go in **peace** and be healed of your affliction." Mark 5:33-34

By His peace we become children of God

"But as many as received Him, to them He gave the right to become **children** of God, even to those who believe in His name, who were born, not of blood nor of the will of the flesh nor of the will of man, but of God." John 1:12-13

"'We have Abraham for our father'; for I say to you that from these stones God is able to raise up **children** to Abraham." Matthew 3:8-9

"Therefore everyone who confesses Me before men, I will also confess him before My Father who is in heaven. But whoever denies Me before men, I will also deny him before My Father who is in heaven. Do not think that I came to bring peace on the earth; I did not come to bring **peace**, but a sword. For I came to SET A MAN AGAINST HIS **FATHER**, AND A **DAUGHTER** AGAINST HER **MOTHER**, AND A **DAUGHTER-IN-LAW** AGAINST HER **MOTHER-IN-LAW**; and A MAN'S ENEMIES WILL BE THE MEMBERS OF HIS HOUSEHOLD. He who loves **father** or **mother** more than Me is not worthy of Me; and he who loves **son** or **daughter** more than Me is not worthy of Me. And he who does not take his cross and follow after Me is not worthy of Me. He who has found his life will lose it, and he who has lost his life for My sake will find it." Matthew 10:32-39

"Truly I say to you, unless you are converted and become like **children**, you will not enter the kingdom of heaven." Matthew 18:3

Christ gives us peace through the Holy Spirit

"So Jesus said to them again, "**Peace** be with you; as the Father has sent Me, I also send you. And when He had said this, He breathed on them and said to them, "Receive the **Holy Spirit**." John 20:21-22

"For the mind set on the flesh is death, but the mind set on the Spirit is life and **peace**" Romans 8:6

"But the Helper, the **Holy Spirit**, whom the Father will send in My name, He will teach you all things, and bring to your remembrance all that I said to you. **Peace** I leave with you; My **peace** I give to you; not as the world gives do I give to you. Do not let your heart be troubled, nor let it be fearful. You heard that I said to you, 'I go away, and I will come to you.' If you loved Me, you would have rejoiced because I go to the Father, for the Father is greater than I." John 14:27-28

"Because you are sons, God has sent forth the **Spirit** of His Son into our hearts, crying, 'Abba! Father!' Therefore you are no longer a slave, but a **son**; and if a **son**, then an heir through God." Galatians 4:6-7

We are to be obedient children of God

"By this we know that we love the **children** of God, when we love God and observe His commandments." 1 John 5:2

"But I say to you, love your enemies and pray for those who persecute you, so that you may be **sons** of your Father who is in heaven" Matthew 5:44-45

"By this the **children** of God and the **children** of the devil are obvious: anyone who does not practice righteousness is not of God, nor the one who does not love his brother." 1 John 3:10

All peace will be removed during the end days

"When anguish comes, they will seek **peace**, but there will be none. Disaster will come upon disaster and rumor will be added to rumor; then they will seek a vision from a prophet, but the law will be lost from the priest and counsel from the elders. The king will mourn, the prince will be clothed with horror, and the hands of the people of the land will tremble. According to their conduct I will deal with them, and by their judgments I will judge them. And they will know that I am the LORD." Ezekiel 7:25-27

"For you yourselves know full well that the day of the Lord will come just like a thief in the night. While they are saying, '**Peace** and safety!' then destruction will come upon them suddenly like labor pains upon a woman with child, and they will not escape." 1 Thessalonians 5:2-3

"And the **peaceful** folds are made silent Because of the fierce anger of the LORD. He has left His hiding place like the lion; For their land has become a horror Because of the fierceness of the oppressing sword And because of His fierce anger." Jeremiah 25:37-38

"When He broke the second seal, I heard the second living creature saying, 'Come.' And another, a red horse, went out; and to him who sat on it, it was granted to take **peace** from the earth, and that men would slay one another; and a great sword was given to him." Revelation 6:3-4

And His children will be revealed

"For I consider that the sufferings of this present time are not worthy to be compared with the glory that is to be revealed to us. For the anxious longing of the creation waits eagerly for the revealing of the sons of God." Romans 8:18-19

"'AND IT SHALL BE IN THE LAST DAYS,' God says, 'THAT I WILL POUR FORTH OF MY SPIRIT ON ALL MANKIND; AND YOUR SONS AND YOUR DAUGHTERS SHALL PROPHESY, AND YOUR YOUNG MEN SHALL SEE VISIONS, AND YOUR OLD MEN SHALL DREAM DREAMS; EVEN ON MY BONDSLAVES, BOTH MEN AND WOMEN, I WILL IN THOSE DAYS POUR FORTH OF MY SPIRIT And they shall prophesy. AND I WILL GRANT WONDERS IN THE SKY ABOVE AND SIGNS ON THE EARTH BELOW, BLOOD, AND FIRE, AND

VAPOR OF SMOKE. THE SUN WILL BE TURNED INTO DARKNESS AND THE MOON INTO BLOOD, BEFORE THE GREAT AND GLORIOUS DAY OF THE LORD SHALL COME. AND IT SHALL BE THAT EVERYONE WHO CALLS ON THE NAME OF THE LORD WILL BE SAVED.'" Acts 2:17-21

We Have Peace By Knowing We are Children of God

We all were created by the Father, but few have confessed, that we are His children, and He is our God. For what is peace but a lack of enmity with God. But we are at war with God, and live without peace with the Father. For the Israelites sacrificed their offerings of peace, to abate the Lord's wrath and gain His good favor. (Exodus 24:5) But rather than obey as a child to his father, they worshiped false idols and transgressed His commandments. Because they did not act as children of God, He rejected the peace offerings of their fatlings. And His people were cut from their inheritance. (Amos 5:22) Thus He sent His only Son, as a peace offering to mankind. So that all who call on His name, may become adopted sons of the Father, and all who have faith in His Word, will have peace with the Almighty God. For as the prophets foretold, "for a child will be born to us, a son will be given to us; and the government will rest on His shoulders; and His name will be called Wonderful Counselor, Mighty God, Eternal Father, **Prince of Peace**." (Isaiah 9:6) And on that night, a Child was born in Bethlehem, and the heavenly hosts arose and sang, "Glory to God in the highest, and on earth peace among men with whom He is pleased." (Luke 2:13)

For the Son of God brought us the Word, and He ransomed His life, that we may be called children of God. For He came as a peace offering for mankind, that all may be children of the Father. But to have peace with the Father is to have faith in God, through our Lord Jesus Christ. For as Paul said, "having been justified by faith, we have peace with God through our Lord Jesus Christ".(Romans 5:1) And our faith will be tested by the fire of persecution, but by being the salt of the earth, we have peace with God and each other. (Mark 9:49-50) For when our faith is tested by fire, and found to be true, then He will call us children of God. For just as He said to the woman with great faith, "**Daughter**, your **faith** has made you well; go in **peace** and be healed of your affliction." (Mark 5:33-34)

And how does He make us children of God? It is not through inheritance, that we are His children, but only by the will of the Father. (John 1:12-13) For as the Baptist said, "Do not say, 'We have Abraham for our father'; for I say to you that from these stones God is able to raise up children to Abraham." (Matthew 3:8-9) And our allegiance is to Christ, for only by confessing our faith in the Son, will He confess us to the Father. For as He once said, "He who loves father or mother more than Me is not worthy of Me."(Matthew 10:32-39) For we must be children of God, for "truly I say to you, unless you are converted and become like children, you will not enter the kingdom of heaven." (Matthew 18:3)

And by His death on the cross, He gives us the breath of the Spirit. For when He arose from the dead, He said to His disciples, "Peace be with you; as the Father has sent Me, I also send you." And after He said this, He breathed on them and said, "Receive the Holy Spirit." (John 20:21-22) For we do not live for the things of this earth, but for the things of the Spirit, which gives us life and peace. (Romans 8:6) For the Spirit is the Helper who teaches us peace, through the knowledge that we are His children. (John 14:27-28) And now we will inherit the heavenly kingdom, for the Spirit has made us sons of the Father, and by being His sons we are heirs through the Father. (Galatians 4:6-7)

And what does it mean to be a child of God? As a child of God we must love our Father, and by loving our Father, we must obey His commands. (1 John 5:2) And by being created in the image of Christ, and as Christ prayed for those who persecuted Him, the Lord instructs us to "love your enemies and pray for those who persecute you, so that you may be sons of your Father who is in heaven". (Matthew 5:44-45) And this we do know, that all men are children of God or of Satan, and "anyone who does not practice righteousness is not of God, nor the one who does not love his brother." (1 John 3:10)

And now the end is upon us. And the prophets of old foretold, that disaster upon disaster would abound, and that peace could not be found. (Ezekiel 7:25-27) And it was foretold, that the day would come like a thief in the night, that men would be saying "peace and safety", that destruction would come on like labor pains, and that none would be able to escape. (1 Thessalonians 5:2-3) For the Lion is waiting and will return, with justice, vengeance, and great power. (Jeremiah 25:37-38) For He who is worthy has broken the second seal ... for peace will elude us as the world gets prepared, for World War Three... the war to end all wars. (Revelation 6:3-4)

And the angels on high are waiting for His children, for the dominion of heaven "waits eagerly for the revealing of the sons of God." (Romans 8:18-19) First to His temple the remnant of Israel (the 144,000), then to the eleven tribes of Israel (those who entered the kingdom of heaven), and then to the remainder of mankind. But woe to the sons of perdition left behind!

And heed this solemn warning. For the time to become a child of God is still not too late. For the final hour is here, before the Son of Man returns. For the Spirit has poured forth Himself on mankind, and the children of God have begun to prophesy, and young men have seen visions, and old men have had dreams. For we wait in haste for the day of His return. "**AND IT SHALL BE THAT EVERYONE WHO CALLS ON THE NAME OF THE LORD WILL BE SAVED.**" (Acts 2:17-21)

XXVI

Entropy, the Law of This Universe, the Law of Satan (NASB)
$$\Delta S = \Delta \text{ Satan}$$
To Andrew the Prophet
Completed November 2, 2007

"He will burn up the chaff with unquenchable fire." Matthew 3:12

God's kingdom is ordered

"Truly is not my house so with God? For He has made an everlasting covenant with me, **Ordered** in all things, and secured; For all my salvation and all my desire, Will He not indeed make it grow? But the worthless, every one of them will be thrust away like thorns, Because they cannot be taken in hand" 2 Samuel 23:5-6

"Jesus answered, 'My kingdom is not of this **world**. If My kingdom were of this **world**, then My servants would be fighting so that I would not be handed over to the Jews; but as it is, My kingdom is not of this **realm**.'" John 18:36

"If the **world** hates you, you know that it has hated Me before it hated you. If you were of the **world**, the **world** would love its own; but because you are not of the **world**, but I chose you out of the **world**, because of this the **world** hates you." John 15:18-19

"Command the sons of Israel that they bring to you clear oil from beaten olives for the light, to make a lamp burn continually. Outside the veil of testimony in the tent of meeting, Aaron shall keep it in **order** from evening to morning before the LORD continually; it shall be a perpetual statute throughout your generations. He shall keep the lamps in **order** on the pure gold lampstand before the LORD continually." Leviticus 24:2-4

This universe is ruled by Satan

"Again, the devil took Him to a very high mountain and showed Him all the kingdoms of the **world** and their glory; and he said to Him, 'All these things I will give You, if You fall down and worship me.'" Matthew 4:8-9

"For what will it profit a man if he gains the whole **world** and forfeits his soul? Or what will a man give in exchange for his soul?" Matthew 16:26

"He who loves his life loses it, and he who hates his life in this **world** will keep it to life eternal." John 12:25

"I will not speak much more with you, for the ruler of the **world** is coming, and he has nothing in Me." John 14:30

Entropy and disorder, the laws of Satan, govern this universe

"To the land of darkness and deep shadow, The land of utter gloom as darkness itself, Of deep shadow without **order**, And which shines as the darkness." Job 10:22

"But if you have bitter jealousy and selfish ambition in your heart, do not be arrogant and so lie against the truth. This wisdom is not that which comes down from above, but is **earthly**, natural, demonic. For where jealousy and selfish ambition exist, there is **disorder** and every evil thing." James 3:14-15

Only God allows order in this universe

"Thus says the LORD, Who gives the sun for light by day And the fixed **order** of the moon and the stars for light by night, Who stirs up the sea so that its waves roar; The LORD of hosts is His name" Jeremiah 31:35

We must emulate His order

"But all things must be done properly and in an **orderly** manner." 1 Corinthians 14:40

"They are not of the **world**, even as I am not of the **world**. Sanctify them in the truth; Your word is truth. As You sent Me into the world, I also have sent them into the **world**." John 17:16-18

"Do nothing from selfishness or empty conceit, but with humility of mind regard one another as more important than yourselves; do not merely look out for your own personal interests, but also for the interests of others. Have this attitude in yourselves which was also in Christ Jesus, who, although He existed in the form of God, did not regard equality with God a thing to be grasped, but emptied Himself, taking the form of a bond-servant, and being made in the likeness of men." Phillipians 2:3-7

The order of this universe is coming to an end

"'If this fixed **order** departs From before Me,' declares the LORD, 'Then the offspring of Israel also will cease From being a nation before Me forever.'" Jeremiah 31:36

"But now Christ has been raised from the dead, the first fruits of those who are asleep. For since by a man came death, by a man also came the resurrection of the dead. For as in Adam all die, so also in Christ all will be made alive. But each in his own **order**: Christ the first fruits, after that those who are Christ's at His coming, then comes the end, when He hands over the kingdom to the God and Father, when He has abolished all rule and all authority and power. For He must reign until He has put all His enemies under His feet. The last enemy that will be abolished is death." 1 Corinthians 15:20-26

"Then the seventh angel sounded; and there were loud voices in heaven, saying, 'The kingdom of the **world** has become the kingdom of our Lord and of His Christ; and He will reign forever and ever.'" Revelation 11:15

This Universe is Ruled by Disorder or Entropy

The laws of thermodynamics explain the physical laws, the laws of the behavior of energy in this universe. And the first law of thermodynamics is the law of conservation, that energy can be transferred but is neither created nor destroyed.

And energy exists in five different forms: radiant > chemical > physical > electrical > heat. And the highest form is radiant energy, or heat from the sun, and the lowest form is heat energy, or heat from a fire. And energy can be converted from one for to another.

And the second law of thermodynamics is the law of the degradation of energy, that the quality of energy is degraded irreversibly over time. And when energy is converted from one form to another, degraded energy is lost and is unable to produce further work. And this degraded energy is called **entropy or S.**

The thermodynamic process always proceeds, from a system with a high quality of potential energy and a low amount of entropy, into a system with a low quality of expended energy and a high amount of entropy. And the form of energy with the highest amount of entropy is heat energy, and the transfer of energy can be summarized as follows:

Equation 1:

High quality energy + low entropy → Low quality energy + high entropy

And the mathematical representation of a change in entropy is **ΔS,** where entropy increases as a function of heat, which is mathematically represented by **ΔQ**. Thus, where **T** represents the absolute temperature of the system:

Equation 2:

$$\Delta S = \frac{\Delta Q}{T}$$

Thus entropy increases as heat increases. And in fact, many physicists have hypothesized that the universe is fated to a "heat death", in which all energy ends up as a homogenous distribution of thermal energy, and no further useful energy exists.

For the powers of the universe, follow the laws of entropy. And the powers of this universe are governed, by the powers of its ruler who is Satan. And when the fire of the wrath ensues, entropy or the power of Satan will increase, for as it says, "Woe to the earth and the sea, because the devil has come down to you, having great wrath, knowing that he has only a short time." (Revelation 12:12) And when the radiance of the Son returns, His winnowing fork will gather His wheat, and will throw out the chaff of perdition. "And His winnowing fork is in His hand, and He (high quality energy from the **radiance of the Son**) will thoroughly clear His threshing floor; and He will gather His **wheat** (low entropy) into the barn, but He will **burn** up the **chaff** (high entropy) with **unquenchable fire** (low quality energy)." (Matthew 3:12)

From Equation 1:

$$\text{Radiance of the Son} + \text{Wheat} \rightarrow \text{Fire} + \text{Chaff}$$

From Equation 2:

$$\Delta S = \frac{\Delta Q}{T}$$

$$\Delta Satan = \frac{Un\Delta Quenchable}{Fire}$$

And the world in which we live in, is an imperfect image of the kingdom of God. For the laws of this earth are contrary, to the laws that exist in His kingdom. For where there is order in heaven, there is disorder on earth. And where the heavens exceed in all things, the earthly kingdom fails in all things. For King David spoke of the order of God's house, "Truly is not my house so with God? For He has made an everlasting covenant with me, ordered in all things, and secured". (2 Samuel 23:5-6) And the Lord reaffirmed that His house was above, for He said "My kingdom is not of this world. If My kingdom were of this world, then My servants would be fighting so that I would not be handed over to the Jews; but as it is, My kingdom is not of this realm."(John 18:36) And now being servants of Christ, we are not of this world, but are inheritors of His kingdom. And just as Christ died for our sins, so must we suffer for Him, that His heavenly kingdom may be advanced. For as He forewarned us, "if you were of the world, the world would love its own; but because you are not of the world, but I chose you out of the world, because of this the world hates you."(John 15:18-19) But He shall return, for His priests were commanded to keep order in His temple, to "keep the lamps in order on the pure gold lampstand before the LORD continually." (Leviticus 24:2-4) For as the Lord said to His bride, "be dressed in readiness, and keep your lamps lit."(Luke 12:34)

For the realm of this world, is an imperfect image of the kingdom to come, for the ruler of this world is not God, but the ruler of this world is Satan. For when Satan tempted the Lord in the desert, did Satan not tempt Him with the inheritance of this earth? (Matthew 4:8-9) And though Satan would be a fool, to offer this world to a mortal man, the Lord still gave us this solemn warning, "for what will it profit a man if he gains the whole world and forfeits his soul? Or what will a man give in exchange for his soul?" (Matthew 16:26) Thus we are not to place hope in this world, for this world is perishable, but to place our hope in the heavens above, for the heavens are eternal, for "he who loves his life loses it, and he who hates his life in this world will keep it to life eternal." (John 12:25) And before the Lord departed, He promised that Satan would return, "I will not speak much more with you, for the ruler of the world is coming, and he has nothing in Me." (John 14:30) And by our Lord's descent into hell and His rising into heaven, Satan was bound for one thousand years. But Satan was released back into this world, and has ruled it with great power and deception. As it says "when the thousand years were completed; after these things he must be released for a short time." (Revelation 20:3)

And the laws of entropy which govern this world, have a tremendous impact on our view of the universe. For if we truly believe in the laws of entropy, then the only future for mankind is annihilation and death. And when God withheld His blessings from Job, Job succinctly called this land, "the land of darkness and deep shadow, the land of utter gloom as darkness itself, of deep shadow without order, and which shines as the darkness." (Job 10:22) And James spoke of the wisdom which governs this earth, "this wisdom is not that which comes down from above, but is earthly, natural, demonic. For where jealousy and selfish ambition exist, there is disorder and every evil thing." (James 3:14-15) But by God's grace and His loving mercy, we have some semblance of His order, for it is not by the laws of Satan, that the sun gives us light by day, and the moon gives us light by night, but it is by the power of God alone. (Jeremiah 31:35)

And now as servants of God we are taught, to emulate the laws which govern His kingdom, the laws of love and forgiveness and order. For as Paul said, "all things must be done properly and in an orderly manner." (1 Corinthians 14:40) For we are not servants of this world, but were sent in this world as servants of God, to spread the Word of His sacrifice for mankind. (John 17:16-18) And by our servitude, God commands us to be His bond servants, to walk on the earth as Christ did, without selfishness or hatred or conceit, but "regarding one another as more important than ourselves." (Philippians 2:3-7)

But few have followed His commands, and God will remove that which He controls, the order of this world and the universe. For the prophets of old foretold, that the fixed order of this world would end, "'if this fixed order departs from before Me,' declares the LORD, 'then the offspring of Israel also will cease from being a nation before Me forever.'" (Jeremiah 31:36) For as the Lord promised, mankind will never again be destroyed by water, for this time mankind will be destroyed by fire. And the Lord will return and harvest his fruits, "but each in his own order: Christ the first fruits, after that those who are Christ's at His coming, then comes the end, when He hands over the kingdom to the God and Father, when He has abolished all rule and all authority and power. For He must reign until He has put all His enemies under His feet. The last enemy that will be abolished is death." (1 Corinthians 15:20-26) For the author of death is Satan, and the author of life is the Father. For Satan is EVIL, but the Lord turns around all evil, so that all men may LIVE. And when the seventh angel has completed his task, Christ the Lamb will be victorious. For no longer will Satan rule this world, for "the kingdom of the world has become the kingdom of our Lord and of His Christ; and He will reign forever and ever." (Revelation 11:15)

XXVII

Woe to the World (NASB) To
Andrew the Prophet
Completed November 5, 2007

"Fear God, and give Him glory, because the hour of His judgment has come; worship Him who made the heaven and the earth and sea and springs of waters." Revelation 14:7

How easily we forget the woes of the past

"For a fire went forth from Heshbon, A flame from the town of Sihon; It devoured Ar of Moab, The dominant heights of the Arnon. **Woe** to you, O Moab! You are ruined, O people of Chemosh! He has given his sons as fugitives, And his daughters into captivity, To an Amorite king, Sihon. But we have cast them down, Heshbon is ruined as far as Dibon, Then we have laid waste even to Nophah, Which reaches to Medeba. Thus Israel lived in the land of the Amorites." Numbers 21:29-31

"The Philistines were afraid, for they said, 'God has come into the camp.' And they said, 'Woe to us! For nothing like this has happened before. **Woe** to us! Who shall deliver us from the hand of these mighty gods? These are the gods who smote the Egyptians with all kinds of plagues in the wilderness.'" 1 Samuel 4:7-8

"**Woe** to them! For they have brought evil on themselves. Say to the righteous that it will go well with them, For they will eat the fruit of their actions **Woe** to the wicked! It will go badly with him, For what he deserves will be done to him." Isaiah 3:9-10

Woe to those who are unprepared

"**Woe** to those who rise early in the morning that they may pursue strong drink, Who stay up late in the evening that wine may inflame them!" Isaiah 5:11

"**Woe** to those who are heroes in drinking wine And valiant men in mixing strong drink" Isaiah 5:22

Woe to the hypocrites

"**Woe** to those who call evil good, and good evil; Who substitute darkness for light and light for darkness; Who substitute bitter for sweet and sweet for bitter!" Isaiah 5:20

"**Woe** to those who are wise in their own eyes And clever in their own sight!" Isaiah 5:21

"**Woe** to those who deeply hide their plans from the LORD, And whose deeds are done in a dark place, And they say, 'Who sees us?' or 'Who knows us?' You turn things around! Shall the potter be considered as equal with the clay, That what is made would say to its maker, 'He did not make me'; Or what is formed say to him who formed it, 'He has no understanding?'" Isaiah 29:15-16

Woe to the evil ways of our leaders

"**Woe** to those who enact evil statutes And to those who constantly record unjust decisions, So as to deprive the needy of justice And rob the poor of My people of their rights, So that widows may be their spoil And that they may plunder the orphans. Now what will you do in the day of punishment, And in the devastation which will come from afar? To whom will you flee for help? And where will you leave your wealth? Nothing remains but to crouch among the captives Or fall among the slain. In spite of all this, His anger does not turn away And His hand is still stretched out." Isaiah 10:1-4

"**Woe** to him who increases what is not his-- For how long-- And makes himself rich with loans?' Will not your creditors rise up suddenly, And those who collect from you awaken? Indeed, you will become plunder for them. Because you have looted many nations, All the remainder of the peoples will loot you-- Because of human bloodshed and violence done to the land, To the town and all its inhabitants." Habakkuk 2:6-7

Woe to the religious leaders who lead the sheep astray

"**Woe** to the world because of its stumbling blocks! For it is inevitable that stumbling blocks come; but **woe** to that man through whom the stumbling block comes!" Matthew 18:7

"But **woe** to you, scribes and Pharisees, hypocrites, because you shut off the kingdom of heaven from people ; for you do not enter in yourselves, nor do you allow those who are entering to go in." Matthew 23:13

"'**Woe** to the shepherds who are destroying and scattering the sheep of My pasture!' declares the LORD. Therefore thus says the LORD God of Israel concerning the shepherds who are tending My people: 'You have scattered My flock and driven them away, and have not attended to them; behold, I am about to attend to you for the evil of your deeds,' declares the LORD. Then I Myself will gather the remnant of My flock out of all the countries where I have driven them and bring them back to their pasture, and they will be fruitful and multiply" Jeremiah 23:1-3

Woe to those who do not believe

"**Woe** to the one who quarrels with his Maker-- An earthenware vessel among the vessels of earth! Will the clay say to the potter, 'What are you doing?' Or the thing you are making say, 'He has no hands?'" Isaiah 45:9

"Look, they keep saying to me, 'Where is the word of the LORD? Let it come now!' But as for me, I have not hurried away from being a shepherd after You, Nor have I longed for the **woeful** day; You Yourself know that the utterance of my lips Was in Your presence. Do not be a terror to me; You are my refuge in the day of disaster. Let those who persecute me be put to shame, but as for me, let me not be put to shame; Let them be dismayed, but let me not be dismayed. Bring on them a day of disaster, And crush them with twofold destruction!" Jeremiah 17:15-18

There will be three woes: New York City, Jerusalem, and San Francisco

"Then I looked, and I heard an eagle flying in midheaven, saying with a loud voice, '**Woe, woe, woe** to those who dwell on the earth, because of the remaining blasts of the trumpet of the three angels who are about to sound!'" Revelation 8:13

"The first **woe** is past; behold, two **woe**s are still coming after these things." Revelation 9:12

"And in that hour there was a great earthquake, and a tenth of the city fell; seven thousand people were killed in the earthquake, and the rest were terrified and gave glory to the God of heaven. The second **woe** is past; behold, the third **woe** is coming quickly." Revelation 11:13-14

"For this reason, rejoice, O heavens and you who dwell in them. **Woe** to the earth and the sea, because the devil has come down to you, having great wrath, knowing that he has only a short time." Revelation 12:12

"And the kings of the earth, who committed acts of immorality and lived sensuously with her, will weep and lament over her when they see the smoke of her burning, standing at a distance because of the fear of her torment, saying, '**Woe, woe**, the great city, Babylon, the strong city! For in one hour your judgment has come.'" Revelation 18:9-10

The Three Woes: New York, Jerusalem, and San Francisco

The victorious odes of ancient past, are but a remnant of the woes to come. For as the Moabites were crushed by God's hands (Numbers 21:29-31), so will the blood of man flow in His winepress. For empires have fallen by His mighty hand, yet man has forgotten that He is the God, "who smote the Egyptians with all kinds of plagues in the wilderness." (1 Samuel 4:7-8) But He is not a merciless God, for He gives fruit to the righteous, and He punishes those who have perpetrated evil. Thus "woe to the wicked! It will go badly with him, for what he deserves will be done to him." (Isaiah 3:9-10)

Prepare yourselves for His return is upon us, and woe to those who have stirred up His wrath! And "woe to those who rise early in the morning that they may pursue strong drink, who stay up late in the evening that wine may inflame them!" (Isaiah 5:11) For their sins are not from the cup of the wine, but from the spirit of the wine, and its harm to man's mind. (Isaiah 5:22) For the mind of man, is the mind of Christ, and through Christ's mind we know the Truth. But through the blinding spirit of wine, the mind is subject to the deception of Satan, and through his deception the Truth is blotted out. So be sober minded, and on your mark, keep your lamps lit, for that day will come life a thief in the night.

"Woe to those who call evil good, and good evil; who substitute darkness for light and light for darkness". (Isaiah 5:20) For there are those who claim to do good (Bush, Cheney, al-Sadr, Ahmadinejad), and claim to be instruments of the Light, but perpetrate evil and are sons of the dark. And they claim to be "wise in their own eyes and clever in their own sight!" (Isaiah 5:21) Yet the Lord sees and knows all their lies and deceit, and He solemnly promises "as for these things which you are looking at, the days will come in which there will not be left one stone upon another which will not be torn down." (Luke 21:6) Yet they continue to devise their evil plans, and yet the Lord sees all their wicked ways. For it is He who has created us and not we ourselves, and the Potter shall shatter the pots, and their judgment shall be great indeed. (Isaiah 29:15-16)

"Woe to those who enact evil statutes and to those who constantly record unjust decisions, so as to deprive the needy of justice and rob the poor of My people of their rights". (Isaiah 10:1-2) For the day is coming, when the wealth of their oil will not help them, but will bring upon them a great curse. For they have plundered the nations of their oil and wealth, but now they will be plundered for their wicked ways. (Habakkuk 2:6-7) And how can they justify filling their coffers, while so many people have perished in need?

"Woe to the world because of its stumbling blocks! For it is inevitable that stumbling blocks come; but woe to that man through whom the stumbling block comes!" (Matthew 18:7) And by calling yourselves sons of God, you have made yourselves sons of perdition. Is it not sufficient, that you have come from the bowels of hell, yet you drag the souls of your followers with you? "For you do not enter in yourselves, nor do you allow those who are entering to go in." (Matthew 23:13) For Christ is the Great Shepherd, but the shepherds of this age have scattered His sheep. "Behold, I am about to attend to you for the evil of your deeds," declares the LORD. "Then I Myself will gather the remnant of My flock out of all the countries where I have driven them and bring them back to their pasture, and they will be fruitful and multiply." (Jeremiah 23:1-3)

"Woe to the one who quarrels with his Maker-- An earthenware vessel among the vessels of earth! Will the clay say to the potter, 'What are you doing?' Or the thing you are making say, 'He has no hands'?"(Isaiah 45:9) Oh, what irony of ironies! For man in his finite knowledge believes there is no God, but believes he controls the course of his life. And God in His infinite knowledge and ways, has let man believe in this lie; yet in truth, it is He is who creates and controls all things. And "look, they keep saying to me, 'Where is the word of the LORD? Let it come now!'" For the woeful day is coming, when the Word of the Lord will return, and His vengeance and destruction will abound. For He will crush them with twofold destruction, with the woes of the earth, and the fires from the heavens. (Jeremiah 17:15-18)

"Woe, woe, woe to those who dwell on the earth, because of the remaining blasts of the trumpet of the three angels who are about to sound!" (Revelation 8:13) For WOE turned over is **3 OM**, three omens of the wrath to come. For there will be three great woes, for the woes are three great earthquakes ... of the magnitude this world has never seen before. And these woes are just an omen, of the wrath that will come. (Revelation 9:12)

And on January 3, 2010, the first great woe will come, and the sixth seal shall be opened , "and there was a great earthquake; and the sun became black as sackcloth made of hair, and the whole moon became like blood; and the stars of the sky fell to the earth, as a fig tree casts its unripe figs when shaken by a great wind. The sky was split apart like a scroll when it is rolled up, and every mountain and island were moved out of their places. Then the kings of the earth and the great men and the commanders and the rich and the strong and every slave and free man hid themselves in the caves and among the rocks of the mountains; and they said to the mountains and to the rocks, 'Fall on us and hide us from the presence of Him who sits on the throne, and from the wrath of the Lamb; for the great day of their wrath has come, and who is able to stand?'" (Revelation 6:12-17) And read the Quatrain about the *New City*, "Earth-shaking fire from the center of the earth. Will cause the towers around the New City to shake." (Michel de Nostradame, *Les Propheties,* Century 1, Quatrain 87) For on that fateful day, New York City will sustain a cataclysmic earthquake. And the stars of the sky will crash to the earth, for our stars are Wall Street and our economy. Then the world will know, that the Day of the judgment and wrath have come, and who is able to stand indeed!

"And in that hour there was a great earthquake, and a tenth of the city fell; seven thousand people were killed in the earthquake, and the rest were terrified and gave glory to the God of heaven. The second woe is past; behold, the third woe is coming quickly." (Revelation 11:13-14) And what is the second woe? The second will occur, where His witness will be martyred, on the site where they crucified, our Lord on the cross. And three and one half days will pass by, and His witness will rise from the dead, and the Lord will take him in the clouds, and the second great woe will ensue. For the second woe will be in Jerusalem, an earthquake that will shake the whole earth. And behold the third woe comes quickly, in the modern day Sodom and Gomorrah. For the third woe will be San Francisco.

But the three woes were prophesied not just in the Bible, for the Muslim prophecy speaks of the same. And hear the words of the *Qiyaamah*, the Islamic prophecies from the Koran. "The ground will cave in: one in the East, one in the west, and one in Hejaz, Saudi Arabia. "For they are the same three quakes foretold in the Bible. "One in the east" will be New York City, on January 3, 2010. "One in the west" will be San Francisco, on December 14, 2010. "And one in Hejaz, Saudi Arabia" will occur throughout all of Saudi Arabia. For Hejaz is the western coast of Saudi Arabia, which includes the holy cities of Medina and Mecca. For all three holy cities (Jerusalem, Mecca, and Medina) lie along a fault line,

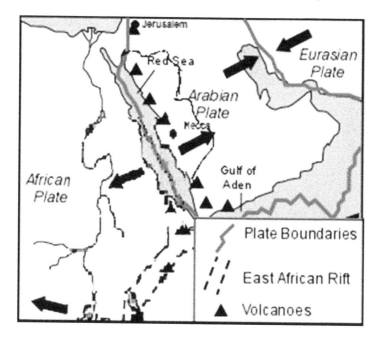

that runs through the Dead Sea and along the Arabian plate. Thus when the second woe occurs, the entire continent of Arabia shall be destroyed!

But as horrifying as these three woes may seem, they are just omens of the wrath that will come. For as it says, "For this reason, rejoice, O heavens and you who dwell in them. Woe to the earth and the sea, because the devil has come down to you, having great wrath, knowing that he has only a short time." (Revelation 12:12)

But though the wrath of Satan is great, he is but a pawn in the hands of our God. For after the flesh and the ruler of this earth, have subjected themselves to the horrors of the holocaust, the Lord in His mercy shall intervene. For in one brief hour, all of the earth will be destroyed by His mighty hand. "Woe, woe, the great city, Babylon, the strong city! For in one hour your judgment has come." (Revelation 18:9-10) For in one brief hour a great asteroid, will be cast in the sea and destroy, any remnant that is left on the earth. Then Satan's dominion will be just a past, and the kingdom of God will be here at last. For who do we fear but God alone? But for now WOE, WOE, WOE the trumpets drone!

XXVIII

The Beast From the Sea (NASB)
To Andrew the Prophet
Completed December 21, 2007

"And the dragon stood on the sand of the seashore. Then I saw a beast coming up out of the sea, having ten horns and seven heads, and on his horns were ten diadems, and on his heads were blasphemous names. And the beast which I saw was like a leopard, and his feet were like those of a bear, and his mouth like the mouth of a lion. And the dragon gave him his power and his throne and great authority. I saw one of his heads as if it had been slain, and his fatal wound was healed. And the whole earth was amazed and followed after the beast; they worshiped the dragon because he gave his authority to the beast; and they worshiped the beast, saying, 'Who is like the beast, and who is able to wage war with him?' There was given to him a mouth speaking arrogant words and blasphemies, and authority to act for forty-two months was given to him". (Revelation 13:1-5)

Modernized version of Revelation 13:1-5

"And Satan stood on the sand of the seashore of the Middle East. Then I saw Bush, Cheney, and Rumsfeld coming up out of the sea, having ten lies and seven nations (US, England, Spain, Saudi Arabia, Japan, Australia, Russia), and on his horns were ten sins, and on their heads were blasphemous names. And the beast which I saw was like a leopard, Donald Rumsfeld, and his feet were like those of a bear, Richard Cheney, and his mouth like the mouth of a lion, George Bush Jr. And Satan gave them his power and his throne and great authority over the US government. I saw one of the heads, Tony Blair, as if it had been slain, and his fatal wound was healed. And the whole earth was amazed and followed after George Bush; they worshiped Satan because he gave his authority to George Bush; and they worshiped George Bush, saying, "Who is like George Bush, and who is able to wage war with him?" There was given to him a mouth speaking arrogant words and blasphemies, and authority to declare war for forty-two months was given to him."

The Beast From the Sea is George Bush

There is a tool used in prophecy, and that tool is known as time. For time proves that a prophecy is true. And Ezekiel proved the value of this tool. For the Lord instructed him to lie on his side for 410 days, and subsequently the Babylonian siege of Jerusalem would last exactly 410 days. (Ezekiel 4:4-5) Thus the prophecy was proven to be true. (Ezekiel 33:21) And the time that is used in this prophecy, states the beast would have authority for forty-two months.

And how do we give Bush authority? By the approval of the people of this country. And on September 11, 2001, the Towers of New York City came down. And his approval rating in the Gallup polls soared, and his disapproval ratings dropped to an all time low. Thus we gave him authority to wage war against terrorism.

And forty-two months after September 11th, was exactly April 2005. And when his disapproval surpasses his approval rating, then his authority to make war would be lost. And as we know following September 11th, his approval ratings declined and his disapproval ratings soared. And in what month did they finally cross? **April 2005.** For "authority to act for forty-two months was given to him." (Revelation 13:5)

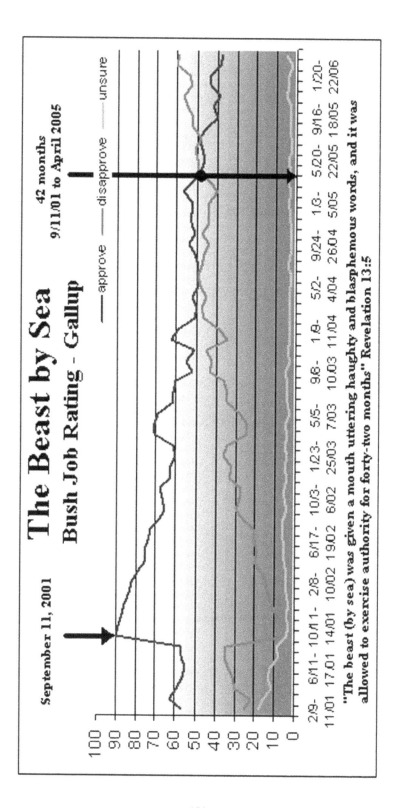

The Beast by Sea

Bush Job Rating - Gallup

42 months
9/11/01 to April 2005

September 11, 2001

—— approve —— disapprove —— unsure

"The beast (by sea) was given a mouth uttering haughty and blasphemous words, and it was allowed to exercise authority for forty-two months" Revelation 13:5

191

XXIX

The Hope from the Father is in our Souls (NASB)
To Andrew the Prophet
Completed November 16, 2010

"You shall love the Lord your God with all your heart, and with all your **soul**, and with all your mind." Matthew 22:37

Our souls are sustained by the Father, the Water of eternal life

"So also it is written, 'The first man, Adam, became **soul**.' The last Adam became a life-giving spirit. However, the spiritual is not first, but the natural; then the spiritual. The first man is from the earth, earthy ; the second man is from heaven. As is the earthy, so also are those who are earthy; and as is the heavenly, so also are those who are heavenly. Just as we have borne the image of the earthy, we will also bear the image of the heavenly." 1 Corinthians 15:45-49

"Behold, God is my helper; The Lord is the sustainer of my **soul**." Psalms 54:4

"O God, You are my God; I shall seek You earnestly ; My **soul** thirsts for You, my flesh yearns for You, In a dry and weary land where there is no water." Psalms 63:1

"As the deer pants for the water brooks, So my **soul** pants for You, O God. My **soul** thirsts for God, for the living God; When shall I come and appear before God?" Psalms 42:1-2

Satan, through the flesh, enslaves our souls

"O Lord my God, in You I have taken refuge; Save me from all those who pursue me, and deliver me, Or he will tear my **soul** like a lion, Dragging me away, while there is none to deliver." Psalms 7:1-2

"Therefore my heart is glad and my glory rejoices; My flesh also will dwell securely. For You will not abandon my **soul** to Sheol." Psalms 16:9-10

"Do not fear those who kill the body but are unable to kill the **soul**; but rather fear Him who is able to destroy both **soul** and body in hell." Matthew 10:28

"For what will it profit a man if he gains the whole world and forfeits his **soul**? Or what will a man give in exchange for his **soul**?" Matthew 16:25-26

"Beloved, I urge you as aliens and strangers to abstain from fleshly lusts which wage war against the **soul**." 1 Peter 2:11

The gift from the Father is hope

"My **soul**, wait in silence for God only, For my **hope** is from Him. He only is my rock and my salvation, My stronghold; I shall not be shaken." Psalms 62:5-6

"I wait for the Lord, my **soul** does wait, And in His word do I **hope**." Psalms 130:5

"'The Lord is my portion,' says my **soul**, 'Therefore I have **hope** in Him.' The Lord is good to those who wait for Him, To the person who seeks Him." Lamentations 3:24-25

"This **hope** we have as an anchor of the **soul**, a hope both sure and steadfast and one which enters within the veil, where Jesus has entered as a forerunner for us, having become a high priest forever according to the order of Melchizedek." Hebrews 6:19-20

Our only hope is in God

"Hear, O Israel! The Lord is our God, the Lord is one! You shall love the Lord your God with all your heart and with all your **soul** and with all your might" Deuteronomy 6:4-5

"You shall love the Lord your God with all your heart your **soul** your mind" Matthew 22:37

"Who is the man who fears the Lord? He will instruct him in the way he should choose. His **soul** will abide in prosperity, And his descendants will inherit the land." Psalms 25:12-13

"And I will say to my soul, '**Soul**, you have many goods laid up for many years to come; take your ease, eat, drink and be merry.' But God said to him, 'You fool! This very night your **soul** is required of you; and now who will own what you have prepared?' So is the man who stores up treasure for himself, and is not rich toward God." Luke 12:19-21

"The Lord redeems the **soul** of His servants, And none of those who take refuge in Him will be condemned." Psalms 34:22

All souls will soon know that He is God

"For the kingdom is the Lord's And He rules over the nations. All the prosperous of the earth will eat and worship, All those who go down to the dust will bow before Him, Even he who cannot keep his **soul** alive." Psalms 22:28-29

"Too long has my **soul** had its dwelling With those who hate peace. I am for peace, but when I speak, They are for war." Psalms 120:6-7

"My **soul** , my **soul** ! I am in anguish! Oh, my heart! My heart is pounding in me; I cannot be silent, Because you have heard, O my soul, The sound of the trumpet, The alarm of war." Jeremiah 4:19

"At night my **soul** longs for You, Indeed, my spirit within me seeks You diligently; For when the earth experiences Your judgments The inhabitants of the world learn righteousness." Isaiah 26:9

"Does the Lord take delight in thousands of rams, In ten thousand rivers of oil? Shall I present my firstborn for my rebellious acts, The fruit of my body for the sin of my soul?" Micah 6:7

He will redeem the souls of mankind

"How lovely are Your dwelling places, O Lord of hosts! My **soul** longed and even yearned for the courts of the Lord; My heart and my flesh sing for joy to the living God." Psalms 84:1-2

"I will rejoice greatly in the Lord, My **soul** will exult in my God; For He has clothed me with garments of salvation, He has wrapped me with a robe of righteousness, As a bridegroom decks himself with a garland, And as a bride adorns herself with her jewels." Isaiah 61:10

"Moreover, I will make My dwelling among you, and My **soul** will not reject you. I will also walk among you and be your God, and you shall be My people." Leviticus 26:11-12

Our Souls Hope to Return to the Father

"The first man, Adam, became soul." (1 Corinthians 15:45) And as the soul of the first man was created by the Father, so were our souls created by the Father. For we presently bear the image of the earthly, but soon will "bear the image of the heavenly." (1 Corinthians 15:49) For the Father is the sustenance of our souls, for He is the living water of Life. (Psalms 54:4) And this world is a dry and desolate place, and our souls long and thirst for His living water. (Psalms 63:1) And the souls of the faithful have longed for this day, and the souls of His promise do earnestly pray, "my soul pants for You, O God. My soul thirsts for God, for the living God; when shall I come and appear before God?" (Psalms 42:1-2)

And who will claim our souls? For the desires of the flesh, are the shackles of Satan, and all hope is lost, to those whom he claims. And the psalmist took refuge in the Father, knowing that Satan has the power to claim, his body and soul and drag him away. (Psalms 7:1-2) For where Satan rules in the depths of his lair, there is no hope, only loss and despair. (Psalms 16:9-10) And why do we not heed the words of the Lord? "Do not fear those who kill the body but are unable to kill the soul; but rather fear Him who is able to destroy both soul and body in hell." (Matthew 10:28) And what gain is there, if you gain the world but lose your soul? (Matthew 16:25-26) Thus we must be strangers to this heathen world, and fight the desires which endanger our souls. (1 Peter 2:11)

And who can save our souls? There is only one, for our hope lies in our redemption through the Father. "For my hope is from Him. He only is my rock and my salvation, My stronghold; I shall not be shaken." (Psalms 62:5-6) And we patiently wait for His promises, and hope to return to our Creator. (Psalms 130:5) Then He will give us our portion, for He is good to those who have patiently waited for Him, and to those who have sought Him. (Lamentations 3:24-25) And our portion shall be great indeed, for Christ has come as the High Priest, and now we may pass through the veil, and receive our inheritance from our heavenly Father. (Hebrews 6:19-20)

And what does the Father ask of us? The world has forgotten His first commandment, "You shall love the Lord your God with all your heart and with all your soul and with all your might." (Deuteronomy 6:4-5 / Matthew 22:37) For we must fear the Lord our God, and strive to inherit eternal life with the Father. (Psalms 25:12-13) For it is the Father and not earth's ruler, who can cast our souls to hell, or raise our souls to life eternal. (Matthew 10:28) And we must place our hope "in heaven, where neither moth nor rust destroys, and where thieves do not break in or steal." (Matthew 6:20) For if we are not rich towards God, then why should He be rich towards us? (Luke 12:19-21) But to those who put their hope in the Father, their souls shall be redeemed by the Father, "and none of those who take refuge in Him will be condemned." (Psalms 34:22)

And now the time has come, when all will know that He is Lord, for He will come to claim His kingdom. "For the kingdom is the

Lord's and He rules over the nations. All the prosperous of the earth will eat and worship, all those who go down to the dust will bow before Him, even he who cannot keep his soul alive." (Psalms 22:28-29) For His people have patiently endured, those who breed violence and war. (Psalms 120:6-7) And when He returns in the clouds, the trumpets shall warn of that fateful day. (Jeremiah 4:19) And when the judgment comes, the world will know of His justice and righteousness. (Isaiah 26:9) And the world will wonder, "shall I present my firstborn for my rebellious acts, the fruit of my body for the sin of my soul?" (Micah 6:7) NO. For He no longer desires the fruit of your body, and each man shall be judged by his own works. And now He asks for the blood of your body in exchange for the sins of your soul.

But when the fire of the judgment is complete, we stand assured of the redemption that awaits. For lovely are the dwelling places of the courts of God. (Psalms 84:1-2) And His people will be adorned, with garments of salvation and robes of righteousness. And all will rejoice in His kingdom, for as the Father promised, "I will make My dwelling among you, and My soul will not reject you. 'I will also walk among you and be your God, and you shall be My people.'" (Leviticus 26:11-12)

XXX

The Spirit of Man is His Heart (NKJV)
To Andrew the Prophet
Completed November 13, 2007

"You shall love the Lord your God with all your **heart**, with all your soul, and with all your mind." Matthew 22:37

"Hear, O Israel: The Lord our God, the Lord is one! You shall love the Lord your God with all your **heart**, with all your soul, and with all your strength." Deuteronomy 6:4-5

The heart of man is inherently evil

"But those things which proceed out of the mouth come from the **heart**, and they defile a man. For out of the **heart** proceed evil thoughts, murders, adulteries, fornications, thefts, false witness, blasphemies." Matthew 15:18-19

"The fool has said in his **heart**, 'There is no God.' They are corrupt, They have done abominable works, There is none who does good." Psalms 14:1

"Everyone proud in **heart** is an abomination to the Lord; Though they join forces, none will go unpunished." Proverbs 16:5

"You stiffnecked and uncircumcised in **heart** and ears! You always resist the Holy Spirit; as your fathers did, so do you." Acts 7:51

"When anyone hears the word of the kingdom, and does not understand it, then the wicked one comes and snatches away what was sown in his **heart**." Matthew 13:19

"But in accordance with your hardness and your impenitent **heart** you are treasuring up for yourself wrath in the day of wrath and revelation of the righteous judgment of God, who 'will render to each one according to his deeds'" Romans 2:5-6

The history of man's heart has been evil

"Then the Lord saw that the wickedness of man was great in the earth, and that every intent of the thoughts of his **heart** was only evil continually. And the Lord was sorry that He had made man on the earth, and He was grieved in His **heart**." Genesis 6:5-6

"Then the Lord said in His **heart**, 'I will never again curse the ground for man's sake, although the imagination of man's **heart** is evil from his youth; nor will I again destroy every living thing as I have done.'" Genesis 8:21

"So Esau hated Jacob because of the blessing with which his father blessed him, and Esau said in his **heart**, 'The days of mourning for my father are at hand; then I will kill my brother Jacob.'"

Genesis 27:41

"The first was like a lion, and had eagle's wings. I watched till its wings were plucked off; and it was lifted up from the earth and made to stand on two feet like a man, and a man's **heart** was given to it." Daniel 7:4

"Through his cunning He shall cause deceit to prosper under his rule; And he shall exalt himself in his **heart**. He shall destroy many in their prosperity. He shall even rise against the Prince of princes; But he shall be broken without human means." Daniel 8:25

But the Lord can control the heart of man

"The king's **heart** is in the hand of the Lord, Like the rivers of water; He turns it wherever He wishes." Proverbs 21:1

"And the Lord said to Moses, 'When you go back to Egypt, see that you do all those wonders before Pharaoh which I have put in your hand. But I will harden his **heart**, so that he will not let the people go.'" Exodus 4:21

"And they kept the Feast of Unleavened Bread seven days with joy; for the Lord made them joyful, and turned the **heart** of the king of Assyria toward them, to strengthen their hands in the work of the house of God, the God of Israel." Ezra 6:22

We must be broken hearted

"The sacrifices of God are a broken spirit, A broken and a contrite **heart**--These, O God, You will not despise." Psalms 51:17

"For I am poor and needy, And my **heart** is wounded within me." Psalms 109:22

"Turn to Me with all your **heart**, With fasting, with weeping, and with mourning. So rend your **heart**, and not your garments; Return to the Lord your God, For He is gracious and merciful,

Slow to anger, and of great kindness; And He relents from doing harm." Joel 2:12-13

"For thus says the High and Lofty One Who inhabits eternity, whose name is Holy: 'I dwell in the high and holy place, With him who has a contrite and humble spirit, To revive the spirit of the humble, And to revive the **heart** of the contrite ones.'" Isaiah 57:15

Then the Spirit can enter our hearts

"Then I will give them one **heart**, and I will put a new spirit within them, and take the stony **heart** out of their flesh, and give them a **heart** of flesh, that they may walk in My statutes and keep My judgments and do them; and they shall be My people, and I will be their God." Ezekiel 11:19-20

"'If anyone thirsts, let him come to Me and drink. He who believes in Me, as the Scripture has said, out of his **heart** will flow rivers of living water.' But this He spoke concerning the Spirit, whom those believing in Him would receive; for the Holy Spirit was not yet given, because Jesus was not yet glorified." John 7:37-39

"For he is not a Jew who is one outwardly, nor is circumcision that which is outward in the flesh; but he is a Jew who is one inwardly;

and circumcision is that of the **heart**, in the Spirit, not in the letter; whose praise is not from men but from God." Romans 2:28-29

"You are our epistle written in our **heart**s, known and read by all men; clearly you are an epistle of Christ, ministered by us, written not with ink but by the Spirit of the living God, not on tablets of stone but on tablets of flesh, that is, of the **heart**." 2 Corinthians 3:2-3

The Spirit purifies our hearts by faith

"So God, who knows the **heart**, acknowledged them by giving them the Holy Spirit, just as He did to us, and made no distinction between us and them, purifying their **heart**s by faith." Acts 15:8-9

"Have faith in God. For assuredly, I say to you, whoever says to this mountain, 'Be removed and be cast into the sea,' and does not doubt in his **heart**, but believes that those things he says will be done, he will have whatever he says." Mark 11:22-23

"But as it is written: 'Eye has not seen, nor ear heard, Nor have entered into the **heart** of man the things which God has prepared for those who **love** Him.' But God has revealed them to us through His Spirit. For the Spirit searches all things, yes, the deep things of God." 1 Corinthians 2:9-10

The upright in heart will glorify God

"The righteous shall be glad in the Lord, and trust in Him. And all the upright in **heart** shall glory." Psalms 64:10

"Teach me Your way, O Lord; I will walk in Your truth; Unite my **heart** to fear Your name. I will praise You, O Lord my God, with all my **heart**, And I will glorify Your name forevermore." Psalms 86:11-12

"Do not lay up for yourselves treasures on earth, where moth and rust destroy and where thieves break in and steal; but lay up for yourselves treasures in heaven, where neither moth nor rust destroys and where thieves do not break in and steal. For where your treasure is, there your **heart** will be also." Matthew 6:19-21

"Now the multitude of those who believed were of one **heart** and one soul; neither did anyone say that any of the things he possessed was his own, but they had all things in common." Acts 4:32

The Heart of Man Comes From the Holy Spirit

"God created man in His own image; in the image of God He created Him". (Genesis 1:27) For we were created in the image of God, and just as God is three in one: the Father, Son, and Holy Spirit, so were we created as three in one: heart, soul, and mind. Our heart is the vessel through which the Spirit works, and when the Spirit works we receive the gift of faith. And as the Lord is faithful to us, so should we be faithful to Him. And His commandment to us is this: "You shall love the Lord your God with all your heart, with all your soul, and with all your mind." (Matthew 22:37 / Deuteronomy 6:4-5)

Our hearts are inherently evil, for they are easily deceived, by the ruler of this world, and they devise evil plans, and fall in his ways. For out of the hearts of men "proceed evil thoughts, murders, adulteries, fornications, thefts, false witness, blasphemies." (Matthew 15:18-19) And the ways of men are corrupt, for in ignorance they say "there is no God".(Psalms 14:1) And their hearts of pride have turned to stone. (Proverbs 16:5) But rather than giving their hearts to the Spirit, they're doomed to repeat the sins of their fathers. (Acts 7:51) For that which was sown by the Spirit, has been snatched by the ruler of this earth. (Matthew 13:19) But all men's hearts shall be judged by the Lord, and their hardness of heart will make it bleed, for our Lord "will render to each one according to his deeds". (Romans 2:5-6)

And as the Lord said, the "imagination of man's heart is evil from his youth". (Genesis 8:21) And because of the evil of man's heart, and because it grieved our Lord's heart, He destroyed mankind by the flood. (Genesis 6:5-6) And the blood thirsty ways of the nations, were conceived by the murderous heart of Esau; and through the heart of hatred and murder, the wars of the nations continue to this day. (Genesis 27:41) And the rulers of our nations, through the evil of their hearts, have ushered in the final days of this earth. For the first ruler came as the "beast from the sea" from the Great Babylon. "The first was like a lion, and had eagle's wings. I watched till its wings were plucked off; and it was lifted up from the earth and made to stand on two feet like a man, and a man's heart was given to it."

(Daniel 7:4) And George Bush Jr. through a heart of evil, was given authority to wage war against Iraq. And the second ruler is the anti-Christ from Babylon of Old. "Through his cunning He shall cause deceit to prosper under his rule; and he shall exalt himself in his heart. He shall destroy many in their prosperity. He shall even rise against the Prince of princes; but he shall be broken without human means." (Daniel 8:25) For Moqtada al-Sadr's heart from Satan shall be destroyed by God, when the final bowl is poured out.

Although the ways of our rulers are evil, it is God's hands that draws the end near, for He is the one who turns men's hearts, whichever way He pleases. (Proverbs 21:1) For was it not God, who hardened Pharaoh's heart, when His people passed over from Egypt? (Exodus 4:21) And was it not God, who softened Cyrus' heart, when Persia rebuilt His temple? (Ezra 6:22) And know that when the Lord's wrath comes, the judgment will be just, for though the punishment is great, their hearts will not repent. "And men were scorched with great heat, and they blasphemed the name of God who has power over these plagues; and they did not repent and give Him glory." (Revelation 16:9)

And what does the Lord ask of us? That men would turn their hearts towards Him, and serve Him in the spirit. But to do so, man must be broken in heart and spirit. (Psalms 51:17) For when our hearts are wounded, and our spirits are needy, then we will know the Truth, that all things come from the Father. (Psalms 109:22) And when we turn with weeping and mourning, then He is gracious and merciful. (Joel 2:12-13) And the High and Lofty One who is Holy, will revive the heart and spirit of those, who are humble in heart and contrite in spirit. (Isaiah 57:15)

And when we have emptied our hearts, the Spirit can enter and make our hearts full. For the prophets of old foretold, that Christ would come again, and we would be one people with one spirit. (Ezekiel 11:19-20) And before Christ died on the cross, He promised that when He returned, our hearts would flow with the Holy Spirit. (John 7:37-39) And now by God's mercy and grace, the Spirit can circumcise our hearts, of the earthly foreskin of this world, and renew us with the heart of the Spirit. (Romans 2:28-29) And having hearts and spirits anew, our hearts are no longer tablets of stone, but tablets of flesh authored by the Spirit. (2 Corinthians 3:2-3)

The Holy Spirit fills our hearts, and purifies our hearts, through the gift of faith. (Acts 15:8-9) For it is through faith that we believe, in the sustenance of the Father, the Word of the Son, and the fruits of the Holy Spirit. And through our faith, we are strengthened without earthly bonds, and produce the fruits of the Spirit. And those who have the greatest faith, will have the power that He promises of. "Whoever says to this mountain, 'Be removed and be cast into the sea,' and does not doubt in his heart, but believes that those things he says will be done, he will have whatever he says." (Mark 11:22-23) And through our faith, the mysteries of His Truths are revealed to us. Yes and even the Truths of the things to come, "for the Spirit searches all things, yes, the deep things of God." (1 Corinthians 2:9-10)

Now all is past and the time is near, for those who walk in truth and fear. His Holy people will rejoice for "the righteous shall be glad in the Lord, and trust in Him. And all the upright in heart shall glory." (Psalms 64:10 //Psalms 86:11-12) For the treasures of this earth are but mammon, for all will perish by fire or famine. But for those who place their treasures in heaven, their hearts of faith are rewarded with leaven. (Matthew 6:19-21) And all who have placed their faith in the Lord, will be of one heart forevermore. (Acts 4:32)

XXXI

The Mind of Christ, The Love of Mankind (NASB)
To Andrew the Prophet
Completed November 18, 2010

"You shall **love** the Lord your God with all your heart, and with all your soul, and with all your mind" This is the great and foremost commandment. The second is like it, 'You shall **love** your neighbor as yourself' On these two commandments depend the whole Law and the Prophets. Matthew 22:37-40

The mind of God is infinite and unchangeable

"Oh, the depth of the riches both of the wisdom and knowledge of God! How unsearchable are His judgments and unfathomable His ways! For Who has known the **mind** the Lord who ?" Romans 11:33-34

"As for you, my son Solomon, know the God of your father, and serve Him with a whole heart and a willing **mind** ; for the Lord searches all hearts, and understands every intent of the thoughts. If you seek Him, He will let you find Him; but if you forsake Him, He will reject you forever." 1 Chronicles 28:9

"Also the Glory of Israel will not lie or change His **mind**; for He is not a man that He should change His **mind**." 1 Samuel 15:28-29

"For this the earth shall mourn And the heavens above be dark, Because I have spoken, I have purposed, And I will not change My **mind**, nor will I turn from it." Jeremiah 4:28

The mind of man is depraved

"The **mind** set on the flesh is hostile toward God; for it does not subject itself to the law of God, for it is not even able to do so, and those who are in the flesh cannot please God." Romans 8:7-8

"Among them we too all formerly lived in the lusts of our flesh, indulging the desires of the flesh and of the **mind** , and were by nature children of wrath, even as the rest." Ephesians 2:3

"And just as they did not see fit to acknowledge God any longer, God gave them over to a depraved **mind**, to do those things which are not proper, being filled with all unrighteousness, wickedness, greed, evil; full of envy, murder, strife, deceit, malice; they are gossips, slanderers, haters of God, insolent, arrogant, boastful, inventors of evil, disobedient to parents, without understanding, untrustworthy, unloving, unmerciful." Romans 1:28-31

The beasts have the mind of perdition

"He who has a crooked **mind** finds no good, And he who is perverted in his language falls into evil." Proverbs 17:20

"The **mind** of man plans his way, But the Lord directs his steps." Proverbs 16:9

"The first was like a lion and had the wings of an eagle. I kept looking until its wings were plucked, and it was lifted up from the ground and made to stand on two feet like a man; a human **mind** also was given to it." Daniel 7:4

"They have said, 'Come, and let us wipe them out as a nation, That the name of Israel be remembered no more.For they have conspired together with one **mind**; Against You they make a covenant.'" Psalms 83:4-5

The Lord counsels the minds of those who seek Him

"For WHO HAS KNOWN THE **MIND** OF THE LORD, THAT HE SHOULD INSTRUCT HIM? But we have the **mind** of Christ." 1 Corinthians 2:16

"I will bless the Lord who has counseled me; Indeed, my **mind** instructs me in the night." Psalms 16:7

"And do not be conformed to this world , but be transformed by the renewing of your **mind**, so that you may prove what the will of God is, that which is good and acceptable and perfect." Romans 12:2

"Set your **mind** on the things above, not on the things that are on earth." Colossians 3:2

"Now may the God who gives perseverance and encouragement grant you to be of the same **mind** with one another according to Christ Jesus, so that with one accord you may with one voice glorify the God and Father of our Lord Jesus Christ." Romans 15:5-6

All will be reconciled, all will be one mind in the Lord

"For behold, I create new heavens and a new earth; And the former things will not be remembered or come to **mind**." Isaiah 65:17

"Then I will give you shepherds after My own heart, who will feed you on knowledge and understanding. 'It shall be in those days when you are multiplied and increased in the land,' declares the Lord, 'they will no longer say, 'The ark of the covenant of the Lord.' And it will not come to **mind**, nor will they remember it, nor will they miss it, nor will it be made again. At that time they will call Jerusalem 'The Throne of the Lord,' and all the nations will be gathered to it, to Jerusalem, for the name of the Lord; nor will they walk anymore after the stubbornness of their evil heart.'" Jeremiah 3:15-17

The Trinities

HOLY TRINITY	Father	Son	Holy Spirit
The Symbols of God	Water (Sustenance)	Bread (Word) Blood (Sacrifice)	Spirit (Fruits) (Works)
The Letters of God	α	π	ι
The Trinity of Man	Soul	Mind	Heart

For there are three that testify: the Spirit and the water and the blood; and the three are in agreement.   1 John 5:7-8

The Mind of Christ is Sacrificial Love

Contrary to what we believe, love comes from the Mind of Christ and the mind of man, and not from than the heart of man. For what is love but a choice of the mind. And "greater love has no one than this, that one lay down his life for his friends." (John 15:13)   For the greatest love of all is that God sent His only Son, and by His love, He sacrificed His blood for the redemption of mankind. "For this reason the Father loves Me, because I lay down My life so that

I may take it again. No one has taken it away from Me, but I lay it down on My own initiative. I have authority to lay it down, and I have authority to take it up again." (John 10:17-18) And what does it mean to love? Recall the words of Moses before Christ's coming, "love the Lord your God with all your heart and with all your soul." (Deuteronomy 30:6) Yet recall the mindful words of Christ, "love the Lord your God with all your heart, with all your soul, and *with all your mind*." (Matthew 22:37-40) For by the sacrifice of His blood on the cross, the triune of God's graces now is complete: faith, hope, and love; "but the greatest of these is love." (1 Corinthians 13:13)

The mind of the Lord is infinite and impassable, beyond the expanses of the universe, and deeper than the thoughts of our mind. "How unsearchable are His judgments and unfathomable His ways! For Who has known the mind the Lord, who?" (Romans 11:33-34) And the Lord searches the depths of our minds, for He understands every intent of our thoughts. (1 Chronicles 28:9) But contrary to the mind of man, the mind of the Lord remains unchanged, "for He is not a man that He should change His mind." (1 Samuel 15:28-29) Thus the words of the prophecy shall be fulfilled, for the prophets of old foretold, "for this the earth shall mourn and the heavens above be dark, because I have spoken, I have purposed, and I will not change *My mind*, nor will I turn from it." (Jeremiah 4:28)

For the mind of man has been subject, to the mind of Satan and the flesh of this world. And the mind of the flesh is at enmity with God. (Romans 8:7-8) And even the prophets, martyrs, and saints were born as children of the flesh, "and were by nature children of wrath, even as the rest." (Ephesians 2:3) And to those who refuted the mind of Christ, were given to them the mind of flesh. And "God gave them over to a depraved mind, to do those things which are not proper, being filled with all unrighteousness, wickedness, greed, evil; full of envy, murder, strife, deceit, malice; they are gossips, slanderers, haters of God, insolent, arrogant, boastful, inventors of evil, disobedient to parents, without understanding, untrustworthy, unloving, unmerciful." (Romans 1:28-31)

And the leaders of this world have the mind of perdition, adopting a language of perversion and derision. (Proverbs 17:20)   Yet they forget these words of wisdom, "the mind of man plans his way, but the Lord directs his steps." (Proverbs 16:9)   And on September 11, 2001, the beast from the sea, through the mind of a man, was given the power of Satan. (Daniel 7:4)   And on May 25, 2007, the beast from the earth was given the mind of Satan.   And the beasts devise their evil plans to destroy the nations, for they abhor the mind of our Lord, and have given their minds over to Satan. (Psalms 83:4-5)

"For who has known the mind of the Lord, that we should instruct Him?   But we have the mind of Christ." (1 Corinthians 2:16)   For those who call upon the Lord, through the mind of Christ, the Lord will instruct. (Psalms 16:7)   And by the mind of Christ, we are no longer conformed to the flesh, but are transformed by the renewing of our minds. (Romans 12:2)   And no longer do we set our minds on this earth, but look forward to the heavens and the treasures above. (Colossians 3:2)   And by being transformed by the mind of Christ, we have become one mind and "with one voice glorify the God and Father of our Lord Jesus Christ." (Romans 15:5-6)

And over the span of two times "time, times ,and half a time" (Daniel 12:7), the prophecy shall be fulfilled.   And mankind will be one mind with the Lord, for the mind of Satan and the flesh will be forgotten. "For behold, I create new heavens and a new earth; And the former things will not be remembered or come to mind". (Isaiah 65:17)   And a new Jerusalem and kingdom will be established.   And its shepherds will feed its people with knowledge and understanding. And the ark of the covenant will be no more, for God will dwell in our presence, and His goodness will be among all nations. Forevermore. (Jeremiah 3:15-17)

SON OF MAN

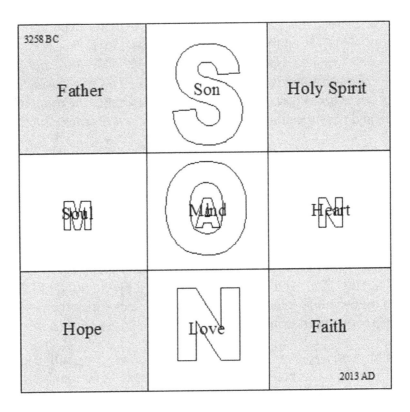

The **SON OF MAN** must be delivered into the hands of sinful men, and be crucified, and the third day rise again. Luke 24:7

Addendum 1

Interpretation of Nostradamus
To Andrew the Prophet
Completed August 9, 2007

Nostradamus - The New City
New York City

Century 1, Quatrain 24

The new city contemplating a condemnation,
The bird of prey offers itself to the heavens.
After victory pardon to the captives, Cremona and
Mantua will have suffered great evils.

911 -New York City

*The City waits her time to fall, Through
planes they plot, a ruthless run. Al-
Qaeda lauds their heinous acts,
Twin Towers fall from Satan spun, (Rev 13:1)*

Century 1, Quatrain 87

Earth-shaking fire from the center of the earth. Will
cause the towers around the New City to shake, Two
great rocks for a long time will make war,
And then Arethusa (the waterer) will cover a new river red.

The great earthquake
January 3, 2010

The quake, the seal, the sixth arrives, (Rev 6:12)
The City's might will shake and fall. (Rev 6:14)
Iraq of old, US the Great, (Rev 17:1)
The war, the third, will end it all. (Rev 16:2)

Century 6, Quatrain 97

At forty-five degrees, the sky will burn, Fire
approaches the great new city, Immediately a
huge, scattered flame leaps up
When they want to have verification from the Normans.

The first bowl
December 30, 2010

And from afar, the sky burns bright, (Rev 15:2)
The fire of the wrath will draw near. (Rev 16:2)
"A sea of glass is mixed with fire" (Rev 15:2)
The world will know the end is here. (Rev 15:4)

Century 9, Quatrain 92

The king will want to enter the new city,
Through its enemies they will come to subdue it
Captives liberated to speak and act falsely,
King to be outside, he will keep far from the enemy.

The four horns (Iraq, Iran, Pakistan, Libya)
The beast - Moqtada al-Sadr

The anti-Christ will want to come, (Rev 13:12) But through the horns of four they fight. (Dan 8:22) The four will send their serpents here, (Dan 8:24) The beast will stay, afar from sight. (Dan 8:23)

Century 10, Quatrain 49

Garden of the world near the new city,
In the path of the hollow mountains,
It will be seized and plunged into the Vat,
Drinking by force the waters poisoned by sulfur.

August 17, 2013
The Millstone
THE END

The mighty Judge will lift a weight, (Rev 18:21)
A stone, a star, one hundred wide.
That He will cast into the sea,
And not a soul, can hope to hide. (Rev 18:23)

Addendum 2
Qiyaamah, the Final Signs from Islam
To Andrew the Prophet Completed
August 13, 2007

The ground will cave in:	The quakes, the woes, the three will come.	*Rev 9:12*
one in the east,	The east, is first, New York is done.	*Rev 6:12*
one in the west,	The west is third, San Fran will fall.	*Rev 11:13*
and one in Hejaz, Saudi Arabia.	The quake in Mecca, God's first call.	*Rev 11:14*
Fog or smoke will cover the skies for forty days.	The smoke will make the days seem near,	*Rev 6:4*
The nonbelievers will fall unconscious, while Muslims will be ill (develop colds).	They all will fall, then calm appear.	*Matt 24:39*
The skies will then clear up.	The two, whom God, had sent, will die,	*Rev 11:3*
A night three nights long will follow the fog.	Then three and one half days past by.	*Rev 11:11*
It will occur in the month of Zil-Hajj afterEidul-Adha	The holy day, the Hajj, will dawn,	
and cause much restlessness among the people.	The world is glad the two are gone	*Rev 11:10*
After the night of three nights,	The two will rise up to the skies,	*Rev 11:12*
the following morning the sun will rise in the west	And then the Son of God, will rise.	*Rev 14:14*
People's repentance will not be	But woe, for Christ is now a Lion,	*Rev 5:5*
accepted after this incident	The fools who watched, they all are dying.	*Rev 11:13*
One day later, the Beast from the earth will miraculously	And then the beast, Sadr appears,	*Rev 13:13*
Emerge from Mount Safaa in Makkah, causing	Mecca will split in two, like shears.	*Rev 11:13*
The beast will be able to talk to	The beast will cause the wrong to fall,	*Rev 13:14*
people and mark the faces of people,	He'll mark their heads with six's all.	*Rev 13:16*
making the believers' faces glitter,	The heads of good, will have a cross,	*Rev 7:3*
and the nonbelievers' faces darkened.	The bad will cry for all is lost.	*Rev 14:20*
A breeze from the south causes sores in the armpits of Muslims,	The bowl of wrath, the atom drones,	*Rev 16:1*
which they will die of as a result.	The skin sloughs off, down to the bone.	*Rev 16:2*
The Ka'aba will be destroyed by non-Muslim African group	Habesha trash their holy box,	*Eze 30:5*
Kufr will be rampant.	They'll curse our God as fall the rocks,	*Rev 16:21*
Haj will be discontinued.	Their holy day will be no more,	*Zeph 1:4*
The Qur'an will be lifted from the heart of the people.	For death they pray, our God abhors.	*Rev 21:8*
30 years after the ruler Muquad's death.	They call the beast, martyr imam	*AP 8/7/07*
The fire will follow people to Syria, after which it will stop. Some years after the fire,	The fires burn on till all is done.	*Rev 16:9*
Qiyaamah begins with the Soor being blown.	The trumpet's last will then be blown	*Rev 10:4*
The year is not known to any person.	The date until this time not known	*Matt 24:36*
Qiyaamah will come upon the worst of creation.	August 17, 2013 ... THE END IS HERE!	

216

Interpretation of the Final Signs of Qiyaamah (NASB)
To Andrew the Prophet
Completed August 6, 2007

We all worship the same God and have fallen away from the tenets of the Father. For we all have failed to love our Lord with all are our heart, soul, and mind. And we have all failed to love one another (Muslim, Judaic, and Christian) as ourselves. And Mohammed was a true prophet, for his words of the prophecy are true. However, the Lord holds this against the Islamic and the Judaic faiths, that they have failed to acknowledge that Christ the Lamb was not a prophet, but the Son of God who came down to this earth two thousand years ago to save mankind. The Father created us all, and thus we all will return to Him. But remember this, that no one can return to the Father, except through His Son Jesus Christ our Lord. And now you will see, by His miraculous return, that He is our Lord and God. So bow to your knees and give glory to Him on high for we all worship the same God!

"The ground will cave in:" These are the three woes prophesied of in Revelation. They are the three earthquakes that will cause great calamity on the earth and its inhabitants. "The second woe is past; behold, the third woe is coming quickly." (Revelation 11:14)

"One in the east" New York City, the first woe, will fall on January 3, 2010 at 12 AM EST. "I looked when He broke the sixth seal, and there was a great earthquake" (Revelation 6:12) The world economy will be destroyed by the collapse of Wall Street, the financial center of the world. "The stars of the sky fell to the earth, as a fig tree casts its unripe figs when shaken by a great wind." (Revelation 6:13)

"One in the west" This city, the third woe, is San Francisco which will fall on December 14, 2010. "The third woe is coming quickly." (Revelation 11:14)

"and one in Hejaz, Saudi Arabia" This is the western region of Saudi Arabia which is known for its Islamic holy cities, Mecca and Medina. The three holy cities, including Jerusalem, all lie along the

Dead Sea Rift and the Arabian Tectonic Plate. Thus, the whole region from Jerusalem and along the entire west coast of Saudi Arabia will sustain a catastrophic earthquake! "And in that hour there was a great earthquake, and a tenth of the city fell." (Revelation 11:13)

"Fog or smoke will cover the skies for forty days." Fog or smoke will cover the skies over Jerusalem for forty days from .... until ....

"The nonbelievers will fall unconscious. While Muslims will be ill." People in the region will be ill from smoke inhalation.

"The skies will clear up." The skies will clear up on ... the date the two witnesses are assassinated by Moqtada al-Sadr's Mahdi army. "When they have finished their testimony, the beast that comes up out of the abyss will make war with them, and overcome them and kill them." (Revelation 11:7)

"A night three nights long will follow the fog." There will be a period of 3 ½ days following the death of the two witnesses, and their bodies will be left in the streets of Jerusalem. "And their dead bodies will lie in the street of the great city which mystically is called Sodom and Egypt, where also their Lord was crucified. Those from the peoples and tribes and tongues and nations will look at their dead bodies for three and a half days, and will not permit their dead bodies to be laid in a tomb." (Revelation 11:8-9)

"and cause much restlessness among the people." There will be restlessness as many celebrate the death of the two witnesses, but many others know the impending judgment of God is coming. "And those who dwell on the earth will rejoice over them and celebrate; and they will send gifts to one another, because these two prophets tormented those who dwell on the earth." (Revelation 11:10)

"After the night of three nights the following morning the sun will rise in the west." On ... the Son of God (the sun) will rise in the Clouds, not from the east, but from the west and will place His righteous judgment on those left behind. "And they heard a loud voice from heaven saying to them, "Come up here." Then they went up into heaven in the cloud, and their enemies watched them." (Revelation 11:12)

"People's repentance will not be accepted after this incident." Woe to the souls left behind to face the judgment! "seven thousand people were killed in the earthquake, and the rest were terrified and gave glory to the God of heaven." (Revelation 11:13)

"One day later, the Beast from the earth will miraculously emerge from Mount Safaa in Makkah, causing a split in the ground." The beast from the earth is Moqtada al-Sadr, the Ayatollah of Iraq, and he will arise to power the day after in Mecca. "Then I saw another beast coming up out of the earth; and he had two horns like a lamb and he spoke as a dragon." (Revelation 13:11)

"The beast will be able to talk to people and mark the faces of people, making the believers' face glitter and nonbelievers' faces darkened." He forces those who worship the beast to take the mark of the beast. "If anyone worships the beast and his image, and receives a mark on his forehead or on his hand." (Revelation 14:9)

"A breeze from the south causes sores in the armpits of Muslims, which they will die as a result." A nuclear holocaust will ensue, and the populace will die as a result of the immediate effects of the blast and radiation. "So the first angel went and poured out his bowl on the earth; and it became a loathsome and malignant sore on the people who had the mark of the beast and who worshiped his image." (Revelation 16:2)

"The Ka-aba will be destroyed by non-Muslim African group." The Ka-aba will be destroyed by the Habesha. "Persia, Ethiopia and Put with them, all of them with shield and helmet; Gomer with all its troops; Beth-togarmah from the remote parts of the north with all its troops—many peoples with you." (Ezekiel 38:5-6)

"Kufr (unrest) will be rampant" Despite all the miracles of Christ's return (the miraculous return of Christ the King in the clouds, and the raising of the 144,000), the Lord will harden the hearts of many, so that they may receive their just punishment. "And they blasphemed the name of God who has the power over these plagues, and they did not repent so as to give Him glory." (Revelation 16:9)

"Haj will be discontinued" There will be no more pilgrimage to Mecca because it will be destroyed, and earth will be in utter mayhem.

"The Qur'an will be lifted from the heart of the people, 30 years after the ruler Muquad's death." Many Muslim's will realize that Christ the Lamb was here as the Son of God and now returns as the King of Kings in 2010; 30 years after Muquad's (his uncle, Mohammed Baqir) was killed in 1980 after calling for an Iranian style Islamic state. They will realize that the Christ was the Son of God who walked on this earth.

"The fire will follow people to Syria, after which it will stop." The nuclear holocaust will annihilate people up to the region of Syria. "there came hail and fire, mixed with blood, and they were thrown to the earth; and a third of the earth was burned up, and a third of the trees were burned up, and all the green grass was burned up." (Revelation 8:7)

"Some years after the fire, Qiyaamah begins with the Soor (trumpet) being blown." The final trumpet will precede the final bowl of wrath. A great asteroid will be thrown into the sea and within 1 hour, all of mankind and earth will be destroyed. "at the last trumpet; for the trumpet will sound, and the dead will be raised imperishable , and we will be changed." (1 Corinthians 15:52)

"The year is not known to any person." "But of that day and hour no one knows, not even the angels of heaven, nor the Son, but the Father alone." (Matthew 24:36)

"Qiyaamah will come upon the worst of creations." The worst of God's creations will suffer through the final bowl of wrath, the meteoric annihilation of the earth. But God is forgiving and kind. Even the worst of His creations will be redeemed and allowed to enter the new kingdom. "And huge hailstones, about one hundred pounds each, came down from heaven upon men; and men blasphemed God because of the plague of the hail, because its plague was extremely severe." (Revelation 16:21)

Therefore, my brothers and sisters, know that Christ the Lamb has come before to save mankind; and He now returns as Christ the King to redeem all of mankind. Remember this, we all come from one Father. Amen. All men shall be saved.

Addendum 4
Quetzecoatl
To Andrew the Prophet
Completed August 17, 2007

Then the heavens spoke in a crash of thunder,	The end looms near, the clouds cry out;	Rev 4:5
And the lightning flashed above the valley.	The skies light up, the angels shout.	Rev 4:8
The Man turned to look again on Tula, his most beloved city.	Oh Man behold! Look down below,	Rev 4:1
Behold! It was naught but a mass of rubble.	The earth is dead without a soul!	Rev 18:21
He wept there with great sorrow.	The kings will woe, the merchants cry,	Rev 18:11
He clung to the rocks, staring toward Tula.	The earth of old, is soon to die.	Rev 6:16
Then the heavens roared again and shook the mountain.	The heavens roar, and shake the earth,	Rev 8:5
A flash of light struck beside Him and cracked the darkness. Behold! The old heaven and earth were vanished, And he looked into another cycle.	The world will end, to new rebirth.	Rev 21:1
The heavens parted and a rising sun shone down on another Tula.	The heavens part, and in the sky,	Rev 1:7
Plainly he could see the valley, but the city was one He knew not. Magnificent was this Golden Tula!	Behold He comes, on clouds on high	Rev 1:7
The Man was lifted beyond the earth.	Now men can live beyond this life,	Rev 21:1
No longer He saw the Age of Destruction.	With no more war or hate or strife.	Rev 21:4
Gone was the horrible Age of Warfare	The wars will end, the star will fall,	Rev 18:21
He was looking beyond the Age of Carnage!	The earth will hear, His second call.	Rev 22:20
Walk with me through this Age of the Future,	So walk with me, beyond this rage,	Rev 21:8
Tula shines in all its glory, but the metals are not the type we know.	Where Tula shines, with this New Age.	Rev 21:10
Loving hands have rebuilt the parkways, have paved the streets,	With love, the Lord, has paved the road,	Rev 21:2

have rebuilt the temples. There is a great building where books are kept for the scholars,

With gates of pearl, and streets of gold. — Rev 21:21

and many are those who come to read them.

By Light we walk, with Truth we know, — Rev 21:24

Tula is a great Center of Culture.

The darkness ends, and Waters flow. — Rev 22:18

Come with me to the New Colula.

So come with me, Jerusalem, — Rev 21:10

Shining again is My Father's Temple!

The temple is of God and Him. — Rev 21:22

Once more the city is filled with fountains

The river flows, as clear as life. — Rev 22:1

And the parkways have birds of rare plumage,
And those who sing to enchant the listener.
Cross through the parkway to My Father's Temple.
You will see again the inscriptions which today your eyes see, but now all people can read them.

There is no further hate nor strife. — Rev 21:4

Come to the city of the future.

So come with me, the gates are new, — Rev 21:12

Here are the building unlike those we build, yet have breathless beauty.

The stones are jewels, of topaz blue. — Rev 21:20

Here people dress in materials we know not, travel in manners beyond our knowledge,

And if you look, upon their face — Rev 22:4

but more importantly are the faces of the people.

The fear is gone, by God's good grace. — Rev 21:4

Gone is the shadow of fear and suffering, for man no longer sacrifices,

And now we live with no despair. — Rev 22:5

And he has outgrown the wars of his childhood. Now he walks in full stature to his destiny into the Golden Age of Learning.

With faith and hope, and love and care. — 1 Cor 13

Amen. ALL MEN.   Rev 22:21

Addendum 5

Mayan Prophecy
To Andrew the Prophet
Completed August 20, 2007

The end of the world will come,	*The world will end, the end will come,*	*Hab 2:3*
so it is said, so it was told.	*The Lord said so 2 mils ago.*	*Matt 25*
Our end will come when there are no more trees.	*The nukes will drop the trees like sticks,*	*Zech 11:2*
When there is no more forest. So it is said, so it was told by the habo-people.	*The end was told, from old, habo.*	*Joel 2:28*
Kaxon bake xen, well, if it is true,	*Kaxon bake, xen it is true,*	*Dan 9:13*
When all trees are destroyed,	*The trees are dead, the hills are bare.*	*Eze 31:12*
when only the hill remains,	*The end will come, the end is near.*	*Matt 24:32*
then the end of the world will come. The end will reach us. This is said. Our end will come. Nothing will be left of us.	*Our end will come, the nukes don't care.*	*Rev 15:8*
It is said, but who really knows,	*It has been said, and now we know,*	*Rev 12:10*
if it will be a storm or if it will be the sun.	*The nukes will come, just like the Son,*	*Rev 14:16*
which will burn us, which will destroy us.	*We'll burn like chaff, the Word says so,*	*Mark 3:17*
Fast, very fast, the end will reach us.	*Just seven years, says Dan it's done.*	*Dan 12:7*
It will only last as long as dawn lasts,	*And when the star from heaven falls,*	*Rev 18:21*
As long as the sun needs to reach the treetops. Fast it will be and nothing will be left of us. One hour and we are all gone.	*In one swift hour, we'll all be gone.*	*Rev 18:10*
Perhaps a great coldness will come.	*Before it ends, the winter comes.*	*Rev 16:10*
Hachykum, Our Lord, will get our blood.	*A Hachykum, our blood He'll shed.*	*Mark 14:25*
He will gather us all their in Yaxchilan.	*The Yaxchilan, Harmagedon,*	*Rev 16:16*
The gods will bring us to Yaxchilan.	*George Bush, Cheney, Sadr, Rumsfeld*	*Rev 16:13*
All the people of good blood will be gathered.	*The good will be with God the Son,*	*Rev 14:13*

When they arrive, their necks will be cut. So it is said.	*But with these four He'll have some fun.*	*Rev 16:15*
Then when the world ends, there will be nothing.	*The mighty angel lifts a stone,*	*Rev 18:21*
Everything will find its end.	*The stone will end the final score,*	*Rev 18:22*
There will be no thorns and spines, no flies,	*But then, the Bible says its so,*	*Exo 12:25*
no creatures, nothing. But then the souls will come, the souls of the ancients, the souls of the deceased. They will inhabit the earth. They will stay with the Gods.	*We'll be with God, forever more.*	*Rev 22:5*

Addendum 6

Hindu Prophecies
To Andrew the Prophet
Completed August 20, 2007

Vishnu has already saved humanity on a number	*The Vishnu came to save the earth,*	*John 12:47*
of occasions, symbolically appearing as a savior in many different forms.	*His name was Christ, of virgin birth*	*Matt 1:23*
It is said that He will appear again soon, as Kalki,	*He comes upon a horse of white;*	*Rev 19:11*
a white horse, destined to destroy the present world and to take humanity to a higher plane.	*To burn the sinners who take flight.*	*Rev 19:21*
Earth will be valued only for her mineral treasures.	*The beasts, George Bush and Dick Cheney,*	*Rev 13:2*
Money alone will confer nobility.	*They kill for oil and blood money.*	*Iraq War*
All kings occupying the earth will be strong in	*The evil men, who kill our race,*	*Rev 13:7*
anger, liars, dishonest, inflecting death on women	*Are Bush & Cheney, by disgrace.*	*Rev 13:2,18*
and children, stealers, and vial character,	*Although they kill, with greed and hate,*	*Rev 18:21*
rising in power but soon falling.	*The angel's star will seal their fate.*	*Rev 18:20*
There will be many false religionists.	*The false prophet, martyr imam,*	*AP 8/7/07*
Power will be the sole definition of virtue.	*Will claim to know who God is from.*	*Rev 19:20*
People will follow the customs of others and be	*Al-Sadr boasts and with his might,*	*Rev 13:7*
adulterated with them. Peculiar undisciplined barbarians will be vigorously supported by rulers.	*Makes young men kill and lie and fight.*	*Rev 13:8*
Because they go on living with perversion, they	*He'll seal their foreheads with a mark,*	*Rev 13:16*
will be ruined.	*So all will know their souls are dark,*	*Rev 13:17*

Quarrels, plague, fatal diseases, famines, drought,	*The angels drop, the bowls of wrath,*	*Rev 16:16*
and calamities appear. Testimonies and proofs	*The bombs will fall, upon their path.*	*Rev 16:2*
have no certainty.	*The ulcers burn down to the bone,*	*Rev 16:2*
	The famine makes them starve and groan.	*Rev 16:10*
India will become desolate by	*The seas and rivers turn blood red,*	*Rev 16:3*
calamities, short lives, and various diseases.	*The creatures high and low are dead.*	*Rev 16:4*
Suffering from cold, wind, heat and rain, they will	*The sun blots out, the winters gust,*	*Rev 16:10*
put on clothes made of tree bark and leaves.		
Being dry of water will be the only definition of land.	*The Sea of Red, will turn to dust.*	*Rev 16:12*
	And though our God is just and right,	*Rev 16:7*
	The evil men will curse and fight.	*Rev 16:21*
And no one will live as long as twenty-three years.	*In seven years, when angels roar,*	*Dan 12:7*
Thus in the Kali Age humankind will be utterly destroyed.	*The earthly realm will be no more.*	*Rev 19:21*

Addendum 7

The Beasts Have Arrived
Revelations 13 (NASB)
To Andrew the Prophet
Completed September 30, 2007

And the dragon stood on the sand of the seashore.

Then I saw a beast coming up out of the sea

having ten horns and seven heads

And Sadr stands and waits afar,

As Bush the beast would start the war.

He boasts ten lies, and seven head,

Because the Euro causes dread.

US, England, the third is Spain,

Russia and Aussies fuel the pain.

Japan and Saudis fund the war,

And hope the dollar comes to par.

and on his horns were ten diadems

And the beast which I saw was like a leopard

and his feet were like those of a bear

and his mouth like the mouth of a lion

I saw one of his heads as if it had been slain,

and his fatal wound was healed

On George's horns are seven sins,

And Donald Rumsfeld claims to win.

And Richard Cheney steals the spoil,

While Bush the lion claims the oil.

And Tony Blair who has no spine,

Despite the war, the Pound is fine.

And the whole earth was amazed and followed after the beast

The Towers fall would start the war,

"Who is like the beast, and who is able to wage war with him?"

For who's like Bush, who kills afar?

There was given to him a mouth speaking arrogant die. words and blasphemies

Who lies and boasts and makes men

and authority to act for forty-two months was given to him.

But Gallup polls, they do not lie,

(September 11, 2001)

From nine one one, two thousand one

Approval ratings fall a ton.

While disapproval ratings thrive,

(April 2005)

And pass them April two thousand five.

And he opened his mouth in blasphemies against God, to blaspheme His name

And Bush who claims to know the Lord,

and His tabernacle, {that is,} those who dwell in heaven.

His lies and sins our God abhors.

It was also given to him to make war with the saints and to overcome them

But now the truth, the time is near,

The Pontius Pilate will have fear,

and authority over every tribe and people and tongue and nation was given to him.

That every nation, tongue and tribe,
Will know his life was just a bribe.

Then I saw another beast coming up out of the earth; and he had two horns like a lamb and he spoke as a dragon.

And from the Babylon of old,
Moqtada Sadr will be bold.

For Bush and Reagan helped Saddam,
To kill the king of his kingdom.
They killed his uncle and his dad,
Two brothers too, while just a lad.

He exercises all the authority of the first beast in his presence

Martyr imam, his title shows,

That we must face, the wrath and woes.

He performs great signs, so that he even makes fire come down

Because Iran will help that whore,

out of heaven to the earth in the presence of men.

Lay nukes upon the US shore.

And he causes all, the small and the great, and the rich and

He makes the Mahdi take a

the poor and the free men and the slaves, to be given a mark on their right hand or on their forehead

A six upon their head or hand.

Here is wisdom. Let him who has understanding calculate the number of the beast

And here is wisdom and no tricks,

for the number is that of a man; and his number is six hundred and sixty-six

The antichrist is 6 6 6!!!

Addendum 8

ECNARONGI
To Andrew the Prophet
Completed October 3, 2007

I am the great Sophia.
I am the founder of this world you live in.
I did not know it, but in its power I created this.
Once I created the beast, the wheels were put in motion.
I could not stop them, so now by His grace, the end will come.
From its barren womb, I will pay the price.
I am the harlot on the beast and I will go to perdition.
And I will be known forever as the Great Babylon.

It was here before the world began.
The Father knew it, yet I was blind to it.
And in that way, it created itself.
And through it the legions were created.
And through them, our leaders, the beasts, now rule.
And they now think they are first, but in the end they will be last.
For this has cursed man since man was created.
And it has veiled man from the truth since the days of GOG.
Yet, the Father used it as a tool to deceive the rulers.
And from it, the nations were seeded.

It is the root of all evil.
It opposes the Father, yet the Father created it.
And though it hurts mankind, it also helps mankind.
For it was created to complete the Father's plan.
Through it, the legions would deceive themselves.
They would lose their power to mankind because of it.
And mankind through it, would gain much power.
And in the end, it will be abolished, and all will know what it is.

It has created great wars.
It claims to know who God is.
It has caused men to descend to hell.
Yet, in the end, it will bring all people back to the Father.

You claim it is bliss,
Yet its name gives birth to its offspring, Hate and Fear.
It should be hated and feared more than death,
For it has made us slaves to this world and its powers.
And Wisdom is its enemies,
Yet it has claimed even Her, yet it has claimed even I.
For through the fruit of wisdom, boasts its arrogance.
And its strength is stronger than the expanse we now know.

And there is only one way to slay its hold,
Because only when we know it, can we defeat its author,
To know Who we're from, to acknowledge His omnipotence, and
to live in His sustenance.